VALUES, ETHICS & RIGHTS

FOR HEALTH AND SOCIAL CARE

VALUES, ETHICS + RIGHTS

FOR HEALTH AND SOCIAL CARE

Phil Musson

First published in 2024 by Critical Publishing Ltd

All rights reserved. No part of this publication may be reproduced, stored in a retrieval system, or transmitted in any form or by any means, electronic, mechanical, photocopying, recording or otherwise, without prior permission in writing from the publisher.

The author has made every effort to ensure the accuracy of information contained in this publication, but assumes no responsibility for any errors, inaccuracies, inconsistencies and omissions. Likewise, every effort has been made to contact copyright holders. If any copyright material has been reproduced unwittingly and without permission the Publisher will gladly receive information enabling them to rectify any error or omission in subsequent editions.

Copyright © 2024 Phil Musson

British Library Cataloguing in Publication Data
A CIP record for this book is available from the British Library

ISBN: 978-1-915713-63-6

This book is also available in the following e-book formats:
EPUB ISBN: 978-1-915713-64-3
Adobe e-book ISBN: 978-1-915713-65-0

The right of Phil Musson to be identified as the Author of this work has been asserted by him in accordance with the Copyright, Design and Patents Act 1988.

Cover design by Out of House Limited
Text design by Greensplash
Project Management by Newgen Publishing UK

Critical Publishing
3 Connaught Road
St Albans
AL3 5RX

www.criticalpublishing.com

Dedication

Wherever the art of medicine is loved, there is also a love of humanity.
Hippocrates

This book is dedicated to all those who practise the art of promoting health and social care in the service of their fellow human beings.

Acknowledgements

I would like to thank my former colleagues, Sally Riggall for painstakingly proofreading an early draft of this book and for her helpful suggestions, and Tracey Newby who helped source some of the references. I would also like to take this opportunity to thank Gordon Craig, who gave me my first job in social care, from which I built a fulfilling career in both social work and education.

I would also like to thank Nigel Horner, my former Head of School of Health and Social Care at the University of Lincoln, for kindly writing a foreword for this book.

Finally, I would like to thank all my former and current colleagues, service users and students, who have played such an important role in helping me develop my practice and enriched the utility of its contribution.

To order our books please go to our website www.criticalpublishing.com or contact our distributor, Ingram Publisher Services, telephone 01752 202301 or email IPSUK.orders@ingramcontent.com. Details of bulk order discounts can be found at www.criticalpublishing.com/delivery-information.

Our titles are also available in electronic format: for individual use via our website and for libraries and other institutions from all the major ebook platforms.

Contents

	About the author	*xi*
	Foreword by Nigel Horner	*xiii*
	Introduction: why this book?	1
Chapter 1	The importance of values, ethics and rights for health and social care workers	9
Chapter 2	Values: who and what do you stand up for?	27
Chapter 3	Ethics: where do we get our sense of 'what is right'?	45
Chapter 4	Medical ethics	60
Chapter 5	Rights: their role in countering discrimination and oppression	76
Chapter 6	Consent and confidentiality	101
Chapter 7	Conclusion	114
	Multiple-choice quiz answers	*129*
	References	*130*
	Index	*135*

About the author

Phil Musson has had a substantive career in social work, developed through working as a training officer in social services and entering higher education as a lecturer and then a senior lecturer. He has held posts at Nottingham Trent University and the University of Lincoln, teaching on social work and health, and social care programmes before retiring in 2021; since then, he has maintained his relationship with the University of Lincoln as an associate lecturer. Working within health and social care is emotionally and intellectually demanding but also rewarding, and he recognises the privilege of being able to make an important contribution to the quality of people's lives and their well-being. This book, the most recent of his publications, provides students of health and social care with the essential building blocks of values, ethics and rights as a basis for learning clinical skills and building good professional practice.

Foreword

The focus of this thoughtful, succinct, highly relevant text centres on the myriad complexities facing those practising in health and social care settings in an increasingly uncertain, postmodern world. However, its essential themes could equally apply to those engaged in work in early years facilities, in education, in diverse income support services, in housing, in criminal justice, in the secure estate – in fact, within any service pillars of the modern welfare state. All working in such spheres face the daily tension between desiring to do what seems intuitively right for the citizen, the patient, the child, or the service user in front of them, alongside an awareness of the policies, procedures, regulations, codes, protocols and budgetary considerations that all combine to determine what actually can be done. Sometimes this tension is minimal – what is wanted to be done broadly aligns with what is right to be done, and what indeed is possible to be done. But this is certainly not always so, and it is in this space of uncertainty and complexity that this book has the most to offer the reader.

Over a number of years at the University of Lincoln I had the pleasure of teaching an advanced social work theory module with Phil Musson. We worked with students on the premise that all health and social care professions are Enlightenment projects, progressively affirming the primacy of scientific rationality over superstition and prejudice in bringing solutions to societal problems.

Such "progress" can be seen to have replaced the label of 'lunacy' with concern for those with mental health challenges, and equally to have replaced the stigma of 'imbecility' with recognition of neurodiversity. During the recent Covid-19 pandemic, the *leitmotif*, the rationale for all government action was to 'follow the science.' However, the inexorable march of rationality has produced checklists and formulae to be applied in scenarios which are often too complex for such reductive decision-making to be sufficiently meaningful or robust. In the Victorian era, James Clerk Maxwell pithily suggested that *'...the whole system of civilised life may be symbolised by a foot rule, a set of weights and a clock'* (Maxwell, 1872, p 75). In the twenty-first century, this desire to reduce everything to what is standardised, and measurable, linked to stated outcomes, targets and key performance indicators, has led to bureaucratic systems that encourage moral ambivalence and ethical blindness (Bauman, 1994). Data is fed into the machine, which produces an answer: *'the computer says ....?'*

However, as is shown by every serious case review following a child's death, by every inquiry into malpractice or maltreatment in health and care settings, following rules is never enough. What is required from all professionals is a constant, vigilant recognition of not only their liability, and their accountability but, quintessentially, their *responsibility,* particularly when making judgements in non-routine situations. It is axiomatic that the more uncertain the situation, the more practitioners will seek to manage their anxiety by pushing decisions upstairs - *'that is beyond my pay grade'* – or by seeking certainties through immutable rules.

However, as Stevenson (2013, p 116) rightly observed, *'moral absolutes can be reassuring, apparently giving a framework for certainties,'* but they need to be treated with suitable scepticism. Simple systems may appear reassuring, but they are contrary to the principles of person centred, personalised, individualised, co-produced, culturally sensitive practice. All health and social care practice is necessarily delivered in uncertain, dancing landscapes, and this book helps the professional traveller locate themselves and their work within the terrain by considering the fundamental tenets of that underpin good practice.

The text takes the reader through the recent crises in care systems, be they abuses in the Mid Staffordshire NHS Foundation Trust, the Winterbourne View Care Home, the contaminated Blood Inquiry, and the Post Office Scandal. These exemplify systems that go wrong, that systematically commit abuses or that omit to protect and that become unable to correct errors through reflective feedback loops. They become stuck in their own toxic dysfunction. By taking the reader through an exploration of values, ethics and rights – and responsibilities – as illustrated via a broad range of case scenario dilemmas, the learner becomes increasingly familiar with Kant and Utlitarianism, with Existential and Humanistic ethics, with medical ethics and the principles of non-malifcience and beneficence, and with consent and confidentiality. Ultimately, this book is an invaluable aid to our collective quest of producing professionally curious practitioners, with emerging practice wisdom, best placed to creative and shape the much-needed health and social care landscapes of the future. I hope you enjoy reading and learning from it as much I indeed have.

Nigel Horner
Visiting Professor for Social Work and
Interprofessional Education
University of Lincoln

References

Bauman, Z (1994) *Alone Again: Ethics After Certainty*. London: Demos.

Stevenson, O (2013) *Reflections on a Life in Social Work*. Buckingham: Hinton House.

Maxwell, JC (1872) *The Theory of Heat*. London.

Introduction: why this book?

In considering writing a book on values, ethics and rights for practitioners and students working or seeking to work in the numerous occupations within the health and social care professions, the question of why this book is necessary arises. It may be obvious that appropriate values, a basic understanding of ethics and a knowledge of patients' rights are fundamental requirements for health and social care workers, but I want to do more than simply assert this truism. Before I explore these concepts in detail, I want to examine why they are fundamental to good practice and what practitioners can do to retain their efficacy though the rigour of practice during the course of a career.

Practitioners in health and social care occupations, including nurses, rightly enjoy accolades from the public they work so hard to serve, as exemplified by the 'Thursday evening applause' during the Covid-19 pandemic. The nature of the work carried out by such practitioners is emotionally, physically and intellectually demanding, and the well-documented poor workforce planning and long-term chronic underfunding of social care have exacerbated stress levels across a range of occupations that make up the workforce. We regularly hear of 'bed blocking' causing delays in admissions to accident and emergency departments, despite the best efforts of those who strive to put patients first. It seems as if the working environment in such places is consistently subject to a high level of pressure rather than a constant ebb and flow that would better enable the management of stress in demanding occupations. The desire to 'do the best' for your patients and clients is challenged in such pressured working environments. How does such a desire survive intact in such conditions? We will explore that question in this book – but, sadly, sometimes it does not.

Examples of bad practice

Occasionally, examples of poor and abusive practice come to light in health and social care settings, sometimes through undercover reporting or personal testimonies from patients, clients or relatives. Such examples are not solely the product of highly stressed working environments, such as the example given in the previous paragraph. Indeed, it is not my understanding that there is any causal link between stressful working environments and poor or abusive practice – or my intention to make any such link – although there may be instances where poor or abusive practice does occur in stressful working environments, albeit not purely because of the stress. Other forces are at play. As this book will strive to assert, the main factor is the absence or diminution of appropriate values, ethics and the upholding of people's rights. I am not including poor or abusive practice resulting from incompetent clinical skills, as this is not within the remit of this book. An appropriate example of the type of poor, abusive practice occurred at Winterbourne View, a private residential hospital for people with learning difficulties. A former member of staff had 'whistle blown' his concerns about the treatment of some of the patients but these were not acted upon. However, in 2011 a reporter for the BBC's *Panorama* programme went undercover as a care worker and secretly filmed some of what he saw. His investigation resulted in six care staff being gaoled and five more receiving suspended sentences for what Bristol's Crown Court judge, Neil Ford, described as *'cruel, callous and degrading treatment'* that had triggered *'widespread feelings of revulsion'* in those who watched the *Panorama* programme. The 11 defendants – nine support workers and two nurses – admitted to 38 charges of either neglect or ill-treatment of five people in their care with severe learning difficulties. See the *Winterbourne View NHS Final Report* (Department of Health, 2014) for key findings and recommendations.

I am not suggesting that examples such as the scandal at Winterbourne View are common within health and social care settings, but this is not a one-off event. Indeed, it is acknowledged within the sector that in situations where there are vulnerable people being cared for, a level of independent scrutiny by standard-setting bodies is required as a safeguard to help maintain the quality of care – and this is not restricted to institutional settings. When I taught the topic of values, ethics and rights to students studying for a degree in health and social care, I showed a clip of the *Panorama* programme and asked how many of the students thought their practice, with regard to their values, ethics and the upholding of patients' rights, could never fall to the levels displayed by some staff, irrespective of circumstances. A majority would always raise their hands. I would then admit that I could not be so confident and painted a scenario in which an inexperienced worker joined an established team and wanted to do well, be accepted, had their rent to pay and was influenced by a charismatic team leader who 'showed them the ropes' regarding how to manage some patients' challenging behaviours. It is not inconceivable that, in such circumstances, our values, ethics and the upholding of our clients' rights could well be compromised into a situation of remaining silent about poor practice or, worse still, beginning to exhibit it ourselves.

The students were not wrong to be confident about their ability to maintain high standards against any level of exposure to poor practice. Indeed, as one of the admissions tutors for such courses, we always looked for robust values appropriate for health and social care professions in our applicants. However, over the course of study we also looked for the development of skills in critical thinking and reflective practice, essential for the effective self-assessment on the condition of such values in practice, and a safeguard against their slippage. There are examples where this 'slippage' of the maintenance of good standards was found to have occurred across health and social care service provision, private and NHS. *Care and Compassion* is the title of a report by the Health Service Ombudsman of ten investigations into the NHS's care of older people published in February 2011. The introduction includes the following comment summarising what was found: '*These stories illuminate the gulf between the principles and values of the NHS Constitution and the felt reality of being an older person in the care of the NHS in England*' (Parliamentary and Health Service Ombudsman, 2011, p 7). Although some of the complaints cite issues regarding the medical treatment of patients, there are numerous failings in basic care, personal care, nutrition and hydration, and the affordance of dignity.

Another example involved the treatment of patients in the care of the Mid Staffordshire NHS Foundation Trust. It led to an independent inquiry undertaken by Robert Francis QC, resulting in a first report published in 2010 (Mid Staffordshire NHS Foundation Trust, 2010). This triggered a public inquiry, also chaired by Francis, and was followed by a second report in 2013 (Mid Staffordshire NHS Foundation Trust, 2013). Paragraph 23 of the 2013 report states:

The first inquiry heard harrowing personal stories from patients and patients' families about the appalling care received at the Trust. On many occasions, the accounts received related to basic elements of care and the quality of the patient experience. These included cases where:
- » *Patients were left in excrement in soiled bed clothes for lengthy periods.*
- » *Assistance was not provided with feeding for patients who could not eat without help.*
- » *Water was left out of reach.*
- » *Despite persistent requests for help, patients were not assisted in their toileting.*
- » *Wards and toilet facilities were left in a filthy condition.*
- » *Privacy and dignity, even in death, were denied.*
- » *Triage in A&E was undertaken by untrained staff.*
- » *Staff treated patients and those close to them with what appeared to be callous indifference.*

Paragraph 24 went on to say:

The first inquiry report was published on 24 February 2010. It contained damning criticism of the care provided by the Trust, drawing out a number of conclusions, including:
- » *There was a lack of basic care across a number of wards and departments at the Trust.*
- » *The culture at the Trust was not conducive to providing good care for patients or providing a supportive working environment for staff.*
- » *There was an atmosphere of fear of adverse repercussions; a high priority was placed on the achievement of targets.*
- » *The consultant body largely dissociated itself from management.*

» There was low morale amongst staff.
» There was a lack of openness and an acceptance of poor standards.

In Robert Francis's covering letter to Jeremy Hunt (the then Secretary of State for Health), when submitting the public inquiry report, he suggested that one reason why warning signs had failed to alert the Trust to its developing problems was *'Too great a degree of tolerance of poor standards and of risk to patients'*. But how do poor standards come to be tolerated? What is the process by which good standards – surely the starting point for our practice intentions – become eroded and are eventually abandoned? I'm not trying to reduce the scale of the problems faced by the Trust, but doesn't it have to start with an individual's practice, which grows into something collective and then becomes cultural? At its heart, doesn't it have the diminution of and ultimately disregard for appropriate values and ethics, and the upholding of patients' rights? In Chapter 4, I will offer the practitioner a specific safeguard against such erosion developing in practice.

One recommendation in Robert Francis's report was to *'Develop a set of fundamental standards, easily understood and accepted by patients, the public and healthcare staff, the breach of which should not be tolerate'*. It is somewhat surprising to see this, given that there is no shortage of occupational standards, codes of practice, mission statements or written constitutions in any of the professions that fall within health and social care services. I will make specific reference to these in Chapter 1. However, if practitioners are unaware of them, or if they fail to adopt them as an integral part of their practice, they have little chance of being reflected in the patient's experience of the service.

The examples I have used in this introduction are a little dated, and it might be assumed that such examples would be less likely to occur now, but this assumption would be erroneous. The Care Quality Commission inspects the performance of NHS trusts. Of the 219 registered Trusts, nine were assessed as being 'inadequate' to meet the needs of their service users, according to the Care Quality Commission's (2022) report, *State of Care 2022/23*. These failings included factors relating to clinical practice and targets for waiting times, which are not within the remit of this book. However, as the Care Quality Commission is also interested in the patient experience, issues relating to values, ethics and rights are also impacted in such a rating. Practice is always vulnerable to becoming inferior to the standard we strive to achieve because humans are fallible and maintaining good practice requires the deliberate effort and a strong commitment to do so.

Nobody wins when things go wrong. The primary consideration must be the unnecessary anguish and distress experienced by the patients. Then there is the worry and concern of their family and loved ones. The public purse suffers due to the costs of investigations and inquiries. The NHS also has to spend its finite resources on compensation. The careers of staff are impacted, and the public can lose some of the hard-won trust in the service, locally and overall. The medical journal *The Lancet* (2013) published the following in respect of the Public Inquiry of Staffordshire NHS Trust:

It has taken more than two years of deliberation, evidence from more than 200 witnesses, and cost over £13 million, but last week the second Francis report finally delivered its damning verdict on why, between 2005 and 2009, hundreds of patients may have died needlessly and countless more suffered appalling violations of their dignity at the Mid Staffordshire NHS Foundation Trust. The inquiry's conclusions had no fewer than 290 recommendations for change.

(The Lancet, 2013, pp 521–22)

The Nursing and Midwifery Council removed the names of several nurses who worked for the Trust from its register, judging them unfit to practice and ending their career in ignominy.

In this Introduction I hope to have answered the question 'Why this book?' and to have briefly set out why it is vital that the application of appropriate values and ethics, and the upholding of people's rights within the health and social care professions, become and remain integral to your practice.

Book overview

I now want to provide an overview of the book's chapter titles, content and the objectives I aim to achieve in each chapter.

Chapter 1 The importance of values, ethics and rights for health and social care workers

This chapter aims to develop the brief discussion in this Introduction, setting out the reasons why appropriate values, underpinned by ethical principles, and knowledge of and the upholding of rights provide the bedrock upon which the worker's practice and their clinical skills are built.

No one's practice is automatically invulnerable to sometimes being diminished in respect of the high expectations we may have of ourselves at the outset of our careers. Indeed, perhaps one of the biggest challenges to the development and maintenance of our practice is to retain the application of good professional standards in the face of the rigour of practice and for these to withstand compromise through the pressures and demands of the workplace.

The overriding aim of this chapter is to convince the reader of the rationale for establishing and applying appropriate values, ethics and rights, which are paramount in any approach to practice within the health and social care professions.

Chapter 2 Values: who and what do you stand up for?

In this chapter, I explore the concept of values and consider what appropriate values for health and social care practitioners might be. Are they acquired 'naturally' as if being of one's 'nature'? This would imply that there are certain 'types' of personality particularly suited to working in the health and social care professions. If so, what are they and how would admissions tutors know what to look for in selecting candidates for their courses? Or can they be taught and learned by anyone, providing they are motivated to help people? There are some political issues that are worth considering here. In the United Kingdom, we have a mixed economy of service provision in health and social care in which patients can be treated on the basis of clinical need rather than their ability to pay. Yet it is possible to reduce the waiting times for nonemergency treatments by 'going private' and paying for treatment. Can values be held in common by practitioners working in such diverse services? Could there be situations in which a patient is refused a service due to their behaviour towards staff? How do practitioners manage the difference in the standards expected from themselves and service users? What do some of the professions in health and social care say about values and which values feature in their codes of practice? This chapter will conclude with a discussion and an exercise about professional boundaries and a comment on how they may justifiably be exercised.

By the end of Chapter 2, the reader will have had an opportunity to consider what values would be appropriate to possess for practitioners in health and social care, as well as some of the challenges in possessing such values in practice. They will also be able to undertake a self-audit of the values they possess in an informed way and finally engage in appropriate boundary-setting for their practice.

Chapter 3 Ethics: where do we get our sense of 'what is right'?

Most of us have a view about what is 'right' and 'wrong' when given a moral dilemma, but being in full agreement with others in our respective responses is not common. We have different opinions about just what is 'right' and what is 'wrong' in any absolute sense, as borne out in the Radio 4 discussion programme *The Moral Maze*, in which a group of people explore their different positions on moral issues of the day. So what are some of the reasons for such differences in perspective? A review of the different schools of ethical philosophy, and the ways in which each of these influence what we think is right or wrong, offers some answers to this question. Possessing knowledge about these also promotes an understanding of 'where people are coming from' on issues of right and wrong. A practical example involving advocacy and resources will be analysed, exposing how selecting different schools of ethical philosophy at the outset produces different outcomes.

By the end of Chapter 3, the reader should understand how 'coming from' one of the schools of ethical philosophy discussed leads to differences in opinion and outcomes in particular ways, providing insight into the rationale for some decision-making within the field of health and social care.

Chapter 4 Medical ethics

This chapter will consider medical ethics and some of the challenges involved in applying these to real-life situations – for example, the euthanasia debate and the eugenics movement. The chapter concludes with the identification of the school of ethical philosophy best suited to be the flagship of the health and social care professions and how it offers the practitioner a framework through which to safeguard their practice.

By the end of Chapter 4, the reader will have been introduced to the four fundamental pillars of medical ethics and gained an appreciation of how they might be applied to practice. They will also understand and possess the means to safeguard the professionalism of their practice through the adoption and application of a principle of Kantian ethics.

Chapter 5 Rights: their role in countering discrimination and oppression

This chapter explores the contested discourse of rights. It discusses the equal and opposite forces acting on rights and how a legitimate right conveys a responsibility on the part of someone else to uphold it. It then sets out those rights which are enshrined in legislation, namely human rights and equality legislation and how the status of these rights confers rights and freedoms, and protects against unfair treatment or unlawful discrimination by providing remedy for redress where proven. The chapter concludes with an exploration of discrimination and oppression, including examples; it concludes with an exercise and analysis of their manifestation.

By the end of Chapter 5, the reader will have gained an introductory understanding of the rights discourse; their potential to be contested by parties of differing interests; and their role in conferring rights and freedoms and in combatting unfair or illegal discrimination and oppression. The chapter provides an exploration of how we might manage difference and navigate a pathway through the challenges it presents.

Chapter 6 Consent and confidentiality

This chapter considers the issue of consent and its various levels, in proportion to the invasiveness of the proposed procedure. It also explores the complex issue of decision-making on behalf of people who lack capacity to give consent. The second part of the chapter discusses the importance of managing confidentiality competently. It introduces the principles of information governance and how to handle other people's information legally and safely.

This chapter aims to introduce the reader to the important concepts of consent and confidentiality, and some of the pertinent legislation that governs its management. By the end of the chapter, the practitioner will have gained an appreciation the issues around consent and the need to obtain it together with a rudimentary understanding of how to manage the handling of confidential information appropriately.

Chapter 7 Conclusion

This chapter briefly revisits the essential messages of each chapter, which promote good practice in health and social care. It then reviews the extent to which it has achieved its objectives, as set out in the Introduction.

As a practitioner within the field of health and social care, you have the potential to be a uniquely important and precious resource to your patients and the service you represent, so finally there is a section inviting you to consider how you will look after yourself in practice.

Chapter 1 | The importance of values, ethics and rights for health and social care workers

Our capacity for compliance, cruelty and wrongful acts

In 1961, Stanley Milgram, a psychologist at Yale University, carried out an experiment to test people's obedience to authority. Forty male volunteers of different ages and backgrounds were invited to take part in an experiment that Milgram described as a scientific study of memory and learning. It involved a 'teacher', who was the volunteer and who, unbeknown to them, was the subject of the experiment; a 'learner' who, also unbeknown to the volunteer teacher, was an actor and complicit in the experiment; and the experimenter, who was the authority figure responsible for running the experiment. The experimenter commanded the teacher to ask the learner a list of questions to which the learner was supposed to have memorised the correct answers. As the experiment went on, the learner increasingly gave incorrect answers, upon which the experimenter ordered the teacher to administer an electric shock to the learner as punishment for having given a wrong answer. The voltage of the shocks increased proportionately with the number of 'wrong' answers. These were fake shocks, but the teacher thought they were real. Importantly, the learner was behind a screen, hidden from the sight of the teacher; however, the teacher could hear the shrieks and screams of the learner as they received the shocks. Milgram found that, despite the distress experienced by most of the teachers due to having to administer the shocks, all were prepared to do so – and to levels that would have been fatal were they real (Milgram, 1974, p 123). Similar replications of Milgram's experiment have since been carried out in several countries, using male and female participants, all with similar results.

In 1971, Philip Zimbardo, a psychologist interested in how situations affect reactions and behaviour, ran an experiment in the basement at Stanford University in which he created a mock prison situation. A cohort of 24 male students who had been screened to be representative of people considered to be well adjusted, without histories of violence or poor mental health, were selected as volunteers and were randomly ascribed roles as either prisoners or guards. In the actual experiment, there were 11 'guards' and ten 'prisoners'. The 'guards' were given uniforms, whistles and batons and the 'prisoners' were issued with simple smocks and numbers by which they would henceforth be known before being admitted to the 'corrective institution' in the care and control of their 'guards'. Zimbardo and his team observed what happened via closed-circuit TV cameras. The most striking aspect was that the 'roles' were 'taken on' very conscientiously by the participants despite all of them knowing this was a mock prison situation. Within hours of the 'experiment' starting, Zimbardo and his team observed that some 'guards' had begun to harass 'prisoners'. This included taunting them with insults, giving petty orders, assigning pointless tasks and generally demeaning and dehumanising them. On the second day, the 'prisoners' staged a rebellion against their treatment, which was 'put down' by the 'guards', whose contempt for the 'prisoners' appeared to have grown. In response, the 'prisoners' became more submissive to the 'guards'. Zimbardo intended the 'experiment' to run for two weeks, but he terminated it on the sixth day due to the incidence of emotional breakdowns of 'prisoners' and excessive aggression of the 'guards' (Martin et al, 2010, p 687).

The 'experiments' carried out by Milgram and Zimbardo, although different in their objectives, reveal unsettling characteristics for human beings: their potential for compliance and cruelty. Aside from such artificial simulations, there are plenty of real-life examples that show disturbing aberrations in human behaviour. One is the My Lai massacre that took place on 16 March 1968, perpetrated by US soldiers and involving the mass murder of up to 500 unarmed South Vietnamese villagers. The victims included men, women, children and infants. Some women and children as young as 12 had been raped and their bodies mutilated. This event is a notorious example of a war crime. But it would be reasonable to suspect that behaviour that could constitute a war crime is exhibited, to some extent, in most – if not all – theatres of war.

A very different example of poor behaviour was found among some British Oxfam workers, resulting in their dismissal. It occurred during the aftermath of the Haiti earthquake disaster in 2010. An investigation undertaken by Oxfam into the allegations found evidence of staff using local prostitutes on OGB premises; negligence and a failure to safeguard employees; sexual exploitation and abuse of employees; bullying, harassment and intimidation; violence against contractors; and a breach of trust (Oxfam, 2011).

What do these four apparently disparate examples have in common? There is some depletion in the presence of social structures that are usually present, which help us to maintain and support good behaviour. In times of war and natural disasters, it is common to see disruption of social mores or norms, the function of civic society, law and order that in normal times we take for granted. This disruption takes many forms and can result in the coordination of humanitarian responses in which humans can take great pride. However, where law and order has broken down, opportunities arise for behaviour that we would not normally consider, in the belief that we can act with impunity and without regard for morality.

What safeguards have been put in place to protect these social structures that support honesty and decency in public service or probity as it is known? Specifically, regarding the four examples above, were Milgram to repeat his experiment of 1961 today, he would have to seek the approval of his university's ethics committee. He would be unlikely to obtain this due to the scant regard for the welfare of the teachers in his original experiment (something that has been addressed in the format of subsequent, similar experiments). Perhaps the speed with which behaviour deteriorated in Zimbardo's mock prison experiment might have been curtailed if the US equivalent of HM Inspectorate of Prisons were due to visit. The Geneva Conventions of 1949 (American Red Cross, 2011) and their additional protocols serve to protect the vulnerable in warfare and provide a remedy where evidence of breaches by forces of its signatories is secured. Appendix 2 of the *Haiti Investigation Final Report 2011* contains an action plan of the 'lessons learnt' that Oxfam Great Britain intended to implement. This includes ensuring that Oxfam Great Britain's HR practices and standards are publicised throughout the organisation, better mechanisms to enable whistleblowing, promoting women's rights, a stronger emphasis on Oxfam Great Britain's code of conduct and mandatory awareness training about preventing sexual exploitation and abuse (Oxfam, 2011). Of course, these safeguards do not, in and of themselves, prevent instances of abuse, as human nature is fallible and we will err, but they do go some way towards setting standards of behaviour that we might expect were we the recipients, or that we aspire to as practitioners.

The issue of power

The issue of power cannot be eradicated from human interaction. It is present in personal as well as educational and work-based relationships; at its simplest, it is present wherever A wants something from B, where B is in a position to give or grant what A wants and A cannot obtain what they want without B. A could be a child, an applicant for a benefit or a course or a job, a patient, a pupil, a member of the public seeking a service, an employee. B could be a parent, a teacher, a nurse, a benefit assessor, an admissions tutor, an employer or service provider, a boss. Power is also exercised in intimate interpersonal relationships and ideally is shared in the spirit of equality but sometimes not, as in the case of coercive control. The Bs will always have more power than the As, which is why a particular responsibility is conferred on the Bs to exercise their decision-making powers fairly, free of discrimination or prejudice or unethical preference. The A B dynamic holds good for many legitimate human interactions but it is reversed where B abuses their power through wanting something from A, the nature of which is immoral, unethical, inappropriate or illegal as in the case of the sexual abuse of children by adults. This may well be achieved in many such interactions, especially in societies that have a high and established intolerance of corruption; however, wherever this difference in power between A and B exists, so does the potential for Bs to exploit their power using it in an unfair, unjust or abusive way.

A characteristic universally present in the climatic conditions in which exploitation, abuse or other forms of intentional malpractice can take place is a differential in power, where the perpetrator of the malpractice is the more powerful and the recipient is less so, rendering them vulnerable. The sources of this power can vary and are not limited to the A and B examples given above. Examples could be as basic as a soldier being armed and a civilian unarmed. It could be a differential in maturity or mental capacity, as in child or elder abuse, or the abuse of people with learning disabilities, as was the case in the Winterbourne View scandal, discussed in the Introduction. It could be a differential in authoritative power and status, as in the 'experiments' discussed at the beginning of this chapter. It could be based on a claim of superiority in social class by upper- or middle-class people to working-class people, or members of a particular religion considering themselves superior to those of no or different religion. It could be based on racism and prejudice – for example, the American white supremacist Ku Klux Klan organisation that believes Black people are inferior to white people. Wherever there are decisions to be made – be they assessments, judgements, appointments or other types of selection processes, or access to services or resources – a power differential is present between the decision-maker(s) and the recipients of their decision; consequently, the potential exists for unfair discrimination, exploitation and abuse, as a group of survivors within the #metoo movement demonstrated when they gave testimony about their experiences of being predominantly female actresses seeking acting roles, who were allegedly expected to perform sexual favours for predominantly male casting directors to get the role.

Exercise

Think of an example when you were either subjected to unfair treatment or witnessed an example, or were told of an example that had happened to someone else.

» Did the example involve an abuse of power?

» What was the outcome?

» What were the forces acting on the victim that might prevent them challenging their treatment?

» What messages did you take away from this experience?

The field of interaction between human beings appears wide open to differentials in status and power, which need to exist in legitimate form for society to function but also have the potential for decision-making to be rife with opportunities for unfairness, discrimination and prejudice. What can be done to mitigate this? Various tools exist that serve to establish and enforce rules of good and proper conduct in these processes. They include laws, Acts of Parliament that confer powers, duties and rights – for example, the *Care Standards Act 2000*, the *Equality Act 2010* and the *Human Rights Act 1998*; Regulations written specifically for occupations and the activities they carry out, such as the Care Planning, Placements and Case Review Regulations 2013; inspection regimes such as OFSTED or the Care Quality Commission, the role of which is to provide scrutiny of practice and assess the quality of a service; and occupational standards and codes of practice against which practitioners seek recognition of qualification and competence from their respective awarding bodies. All such measures can be encompassed within values, ethics and rights, so it is difficult to overstate their importance to the profession to which they relate and how essential it is that their respective practitioners familiarise themselves with them and abide by the principles enshrined within them.

Ordinary people, like you and me

An unsettling aspect of the examples of shortfalls in the behaviours discussed in this chapter is they are exhibited by ordinary people. We are not talking about people like Beverly Allitt, a nurse who was found guilty of deliberately harming babies and children on ward four of Grantham Hospital, Lincolnshire in the 1990s, or Harold Shipman, the British GP practising from the 1970s to 1990s who was charged with and found guilty of killing 15 of his patients, or, more recently, Lucy Letby, a paediatric nurse who was found guilty of killing a number of babies in her care in 2023. These people were serial killers who murdered patients in their care. I do not profess to understand their motivation for doing so but I want to make a clear distinction between those who commit such – fortunately very rare – crimes and the ordinary people who fail to uphold acceptable behaviour and appropriate professionalism conferred on them by their occupational standards.

We could speculate on the percentage of those who were not suited to be members of a caring profession from the start, or those who have failed to familiarise themselves with the appropriate codes of practice and occupational standards, or failed to adopt them or abide by them. Then there those who were suited to a caring profession, and had familiarised, adopted and abided by their appropriate codes of practice and occupational standards, but then underwent some kind of transition whereby they lost sight of them. What could influence such a transition? We could identify the likely suspects as being workload pressures forcing the cutting of corners, staff shortages, inadequate stress management, poor leadership and supervision, or exposure to leaders or supervisors whose own practice failed to comply with appropriate codes of practice and occupational standards. Other factors could include inadequate codes of practice and occupational standards to meet the needs of the service or the practitioner having such a low profile within the service as to be ineffective or undermined by its culture.

As organisations can rarely claim immunity from such influences, how might a practitioner safeguard the quality of their practice? Perhaps a starting point is to recognise that such influences do pose a threat to the quality of their practice rather than failing to admit any susceptibility to them. The behaviour of the 'teachers' in Milgram's experiment and the 'guards' in Zimbardo's 'prison' may not have been significantly different had they been aware of their potential for obedience to authority or capacity for cruelty, but surely being ignorant or in denial of this would do little to safeguard against such behaviour. Moreover, the fact is that this potential was not something peculiar to these individuals; the capacity for such behaviour is potentially common to all human beings.

The working environment

Your knowledge, skills and motivation to do a good job are fundamental to your client's or patient's experience of using your service. But other factors also affect your experience as an employee and the environment in which you work, and many of these are beyond your control and influence. Nevertheless, it is worth giving consideration to these, as they have a bearing on the quality of your working life. At the time of writing, the NHS is celebrating the 75th year of its existence. This celebration is coinciding with strike action being taken across a range of professions within the organisation, including nurses and doctors. The decisions about whether to join a trade union, take strike action or cross a picket line are central to the application of values, ethics and rights, and a matter for the individual worker to decide upon. However, these are especially difficult decisions for health and social care workers due to the nature of their work and the likelihood of a direct impact on patients and people within the care of the NHS. These disputes are not solely about remuneration but include terms and conditions – one of which is the impact of staff coping with a vacancy rate of over 100,000 for well over a decade (Campbell, 2022).

The Covid-19 pandemic revealed just how vital some professions and occupations are in enabling us to live our lives and achieve a reasonable standard of well-being while doing so, and the caring professions and occupations were right at the top. The efforts of the staff working at the front line in the fight with the pandemic were recognised in the 'Thursday night' applause at the time and it is sobering to see morale and industrial relations having reached a point where doctors and nurses are on picket lines in what is the most serious dispute to date between staff working in the NHS and its management.

As the NHS is funded through taxation, its management is ultimately the government, namely whoever the Prime Minister appoints to the post of Secretary of State for Health and Social Care. The person so appointed can change within the same administration, along with different ideas and priorities that each appointee may have. It will also alter with a change of government, along with the raft of social policies that the administration wants to implement in the health and social care field. The potential for frequent changes of key personnel, both from within administrations or because of a change of government due to a general election, results in the NHS being subject to frequent episodes of turbulence, brought about by changes in policy and their resultant reforms.

A high turnover in the position of Secretary of State for Health and Social Care could mean they lack the opportunity to develop experience of doing the job if they hold it only for a short period of time. From 2018 to 2023, there were seven Secretaries of State for Health and Social Care (none of these changes were the result of a change of government). That is more than one per year on average and could result in the organisation being subject to more instability and reform than would otherwise be the case. The impact of this on the working environment needs to be considered, given the enormous challenges faced by the NHS since 2020.

The Health Foundation (2023) has undertaken some work on forecasting future needs. It calculated that 9.1 million people in England are projected to be living with a major illness by 2040, which is an increase of 2.5 million people compared with 2019. This is an increase of 37 per cent, nine times the rate at which the working-age population (20–69 year-olds) is expected to grow over the same period (4 per cent). Some 80 per cent of the projected increase in major illness – or two million people – will affect people aged 70 years and over. If these findings are accurate, there will need to be some forward planning to consider funding options if the NHS's free treatment at the point of need principle is to be maintained.

Currently, as stated in the Introduction, the United Kingdom has a mixed economy of health care, including the NHS, not-for-profit organisations and private health-care providers. I am not advocating any diminution of private providers in favour of the

NHS, but a significant growth in private sector provision would run the risk of creating a two-tier system in which the wealthy could access private health care and the poor would need to depend on the NHS. Whether such a development would be welcome or considered unfortunate depends on your values, ethics and the rights you think should be afforded to all people.

The people who work in health and social care do not have the monopoly on being caring, but many do have a special place in the caring professions as many of their clients and patients are presenting themselves at a time in their lives when they are vulnerable. The source of this vulnerability may be illness or injury, some of which may be so serious as to pose a threat to life. It may be the result of increasing dependency through infirmity or frailty, or a reduction in mental capacity. It may be through significant life events such as bereavement, childbirth or end-of-life care. Working with the vulnerable confers a particular responsibility on the worker to be understanding of their client's or patient's vulnerability and to have empathy regarding how they may feel about the change or condition that heralded it. Maintaining this person-centred response to the presenting client/patient, and the next, and all the patients to come, continuing to offer the same quality and standard of care, requires energy and a professional commitment; it is further enabled when carers themselves feel cared for, which is why morale is so vital.

Who cares for the carers?

Looking after yourself as a practitioner is of paramount importance. You may think the care of your clients or patients is the most important thing, but this would be impacted if you were lacking the support you needed to do a good job, suffering undue stress, subjected to unreasonable workload pressures, and at risk of burnout and leaving the service. The Covid-19 pandemic presented the health and care occupations with unprecedented challenges across many areas of practice, but here I want to highlight the possible impact of caring for many, formerly well, people becoming very ill. Of course, we are buoyed when such patients recover, but many died during this time, including former colleagues. It is vital that the practitioner has some insight of the support they need to ensure their practice is sustainable and has access to this support. Support might be sourced through personal relationships with a partner, family or friends. There is also an occupational context, found through the camaraderie of colleagues, and more formal structures within the organisation for which you work. An element of clinical supervision should include personal support. There are also voluntary health and well-being counselling and occupational health services. There are formal systems where staff are referred to occupational health as a result of having reached a level of absenteeism often termed 'stage one', but this should be a supportive rather than a punitive process. This topic will be returned to in Chapter 7, where readers are encouraged to develop this insight into their needs as practitioners and invited to identify how they might be met while practising.

While looking after yourself as a practitioner is of fundamental importance, it is also important to retain sight of why the service in which you work exists. You may conclude that its purpose is to serve the people who use it. This may seem obvious, but at times of high demand or when facing stressful caseloads, it is possible to lose sight of this.

The regulatory bodies in health and social care

Having aired some thoughts on a few of the perennial factors that affect service provision, I now want to return to the central issue of this chapter: the acquisition and application of values, ethics and rights through the regulating bodies' standards and codes of conduct relevant to the specific health and social care profession. Such application of ethics, values and rights is paramount in any approach to practice within the profession.

The following regulatory bodies are all relevant to a variety of professions and skilled occupations within health and social care:

» the General Medical Council (GMC) (for medical practitioners such as doctors and consultants);
» the Nursing and Midwifery Council (NMC) (for nursing and midwifery);
» the Health and Care Professions Council (HCPC) (responsible for 15 professions within health and social care). These professions are:

1. arts therapists;
2. biomedical scientists;
3. chiropodists/podiatrists;
4. clinical scientists;
5. dietitians;
6. hearing aid dispensers;
7. occupational therapists;

8. operating department practitioners;
9. orthoptists;
10. paramedics;
11. physiotherapists;
12. practitioner psychologists;
13. prosthetists/orthotists;
14. radiographers;
15. speech and language therapists.

Standards

The HCPC set Standards of Proficiency for each of these professions, in addition to other regulatory expectations such as codes of ethics and standards of behaviour.

The Standards of Proficiency for all 15 professions were revised in March 2023 and this revised version came into effect on 1 September 2023. The revised version for each profession is available on the HCPC's website and you only need be familiar with those that pertain to your profession or occupation, or the one in which you are studying to gain a qualification. It is, however, worth seeing one of the standards of one of the professions to see how they are set out and their scope.

The standard of proficiency for physiotherapy, for example, states:

at the point of registration physiotherapists must be able to:
1. *Practise safely and effectively within the scope of their practise.*
2. *Practise within legal and ethical boundaries.*
3. *Look after their health and well-being, seeking appropriate support where necessary.*
4. *Practise as an autonomous professional exercising their own professional judgement.*
5. *Recognise the impact of culture, equality and diversity on practice and practise in a non-discriminatory and inclusive manner.*
6. *Understand the importance of maintaining confidentiality.*
7. *Communicate effectively.*
8. *Work appropriately with others.*

Let's expand on one of these to see the detail:
3. *Look after their health and well-being, seeking appropriate support where necessary:*
    3.1 *identify anxiety and stress in themselves and recognise the potential impact on their practice.*
    3.2 *understand the importance of their own mental and physical health and well-being strategies in maintaining fitness to practise.*

3.3 understand how to take appropriate action if their health may affect their ability to practise safely and effectively, including seeking help and support when necessary.

3.4 develop and adopt clear strategies for physical and mental self-care and self-awareness, to maintain a high standard of professional effectiveness and a safe working environment.

(HCPC, 2023)

Physiotherapists must be able to demonstrate compliance with these standards at the point of registration, but a condition of maintaining registration is to continue to demonstrate compliance throughout their practice. Applicants for registration in one of the professions regulated by the HCPC must sign a declaration to confirm that they will meet the standard when registered.

The HCPC is not solely responsible for standards regarding the proficiency of its practitioner registrants. It also publishes Standards of Conduct, Performance and Ethics for registrants, provides guidance on conduct and ethics for students on any of its approved programmes of training and qualification and provides information for service users, carers and the public by explaining how registrants should behave towards them if they are receiving treatment with another service.

The HCPC also has a function in approving programmes of training and qualification in the health and social care professions it regulates by educational providers to ensure that the curricula of their courses are compatible with their expectations of potential registrants and can equip them with the knowledge, skills and values embedded in their standards.

One element included in the standards of proficiency common to the 15 professions for which the HCPC is responsible is for the practitioner to keep their skills and knowledge up to date and understand the importance of continuing their professional development throughout their career. Accordingly, the HCPC sets standards for continuing professional development with which registrants must comply to renew their registration.

The current version of the Standards of Conduct, Performance and Ethics was published in 2016, but it is currently being revised. It sets out 10 standards, and states that registrants must:

1. *Promote and protect the interests of service users and carers.*
2. *Communicate appropriately and effectively.*

3. Work within the limits of their knowledge and skills.
4. Delegate appropriately.
5. Respect confidentiality.
6. Manage risk.
7. Report concerns about safety.
8. Be open when things go wrong.
9. Be honest and trustworthy; and
10. Keep records of their work.

Let's look at the detail of Standard 9: Be honest and trustworthy.

Personal and professional behaviour

9.1 You must make sure that your conduct justifies the public's trust and confidence in you and your profession.

9.2 You must be honest about your experience, qualifications, and skills.

9.3 You must make sure that any promotional activities you are involved in are accurate and are not likely to mislead.

9.4 You must declare issues that might create conflicts of interest and make sure that they do not influence your judgement.

Important information about your conduct and competence.

9.5 You must tell us (HCPC) as soon as possible if:
 - you accept a caution from the police, or you have been charged with, or found guilty of, a criminal offence;
 - another organisation responsible for regulating a health or social-care profession has taken action or made a finding against you; or
 - you have had any restriction placed on your practice, or been suspended or dismissed by an employer, because of concerns about your conduct or competence.

9.6 You must co-operate with any investigation into your conduct or competence, the conduct or competence of others, or the care, treatment or other services provided to service users.

(HCPC, 2016)

Fitness to practise

When the HCPC registers a practitioner in any one of the professions, it is responsible for deeming that they are 'fit to practise' in that profession. This means they consider a practitioner to have the skills, knowledge, character and health to practise their profession safely and effectively.

The HCPC will consider concerns raised by members of the public, employers, professionals, the police and other people about a registrant's fitness to practise. When they are deciding whether they need to take any action against a registrant to protect the public, they look at whether the registrant has met these standards (HCPC, 2016).

It is worth spending some time thinking about Standard 9.4 in a little more depth and considering what issues might create conflicts of interest and have the potential to influence one's judgement as a result. Obvious contenders include bias or having an unjustifiable preference based on gender or other identifying characteristics. Where this has developed into prejudice or discrimination, it could manifest in preferential regard or treatment, or the converse. However, there may be more subtle and nuanced interactions resulting from simply finding a person's looks or personality appealing or attractive. There is a tendency to feel more comfortable in the company of those we perceive to be like us, hence the maxim 'birds of a feather flock together'. Such influences have been termed *'unconscious bias'* (Agarwal, 2020), implying that these operate at a subliminal level. If so, it may be difficult to be aware of its manifestation and ways to counter it. One way to reveal this is to imagine yourself approaching a situation in which you are joining a group of people who are not known to you, but you chose one group over another based on what you see. The situation might be joining a group of students at a table in a refectory or library, or joining a group of passengers on a train, or choosing who you might sit next to. You only have an instant in which to make such an assessment. It may be that your choice is genuinely random, but if not then what characteristics can you identify that could influence your choice? Of course, it is not unreasonable to exercise personal preferences, but when working in a professional context we need to be aware of and guard against these influencing our judgement or behaviour and affecting the quality of the service we provide.

Expressing identity in professional occupations

One area of potential controversy is what we choose to say about our values, culture and identity through our presentation. For example, in the United Kingdom exemptions are made for Sikh police officers, who do not have to wear the conventional uniform headwear of either a helmet or peaked cap; this is to allow them to comply with their faith. Initiated Sikhs are required to always carry or maintain five articles of faith. These are: *Kesh* (unshorn hair covered by a turban), *Kara* (steel bracelet), *Kanga* (wooden comb), *Kachera* (undershorts) and *Kirpan* (a knife or dagger). Four of these items may be worn discreetly but the turban leaves the observer in no doubt that the wearer is Sikh. In countries that place a higher value on secularism than individual rights of expression within services such as their police force, these allowances are not made. Such countries include the Netherlands, where all police officers must comply with regulation uniform.

'*The religious neutrality of the police should be explicit,*' said Dutch Minister for Justice Dilan Yesilgoz on 29 June 2023 after the announcement that the ban would include crucifixes, *kippahs* often worn by Jewish orthodox men and headscarves worn by observant Muslim women (Cluskey, 2023). The Netherlands is not regarded as a country that restricts the rights of its citizens; on the contrary, it is considered a liberal democracy that upholds the freedom of religion as well as the right not to have one and opposes discrimination on this ground. However, it requires those employed as representatives of its services to place their membership of that service first and adopt the uniform of the service rather than placing other expressions of identity, such as religion, above representing the service. This approach exemplifies neutrality over diversity and its supporters may argue that it avoids a perception, real or otherwise, of preferential treatment by association with likeminded people or creating barriers in response to expressions of difference. Detractors of this approach may argue that it would inhibit, for example, Muslims applying to be police officers, resulting in a disproportionate lack of representation within a police force compared with their population in the community, and that such an approach is racist and discriminatory. The position in the United Kingdom is different from that of The Netherlands regarding the expression of identity. The *Equality Act 2010* introduced nine protected characteristics (including expression of religious identity), and it is unlawful to discriminate, either directly or indirectly, against any one of these. See Chapter 5 for further detail.

Most health and social care services in the United Kingdom have a policy on the dress code acceptable to them, which they expect their employees to adhere to. However, where employees can exercise choice in what is displayed, staff need to consider their presentation and be sensitive to the message it may convey to service users.

Case study

A personal comment in relation to presentation

At one point in my career, I held the post of a social worker, based in a hospital where I was responsible for providing a social work service to patients on two acute medical wards and a chemotherapy clinic. As a member of the non-clinical staff, I was not required to wear a uniform, but I did carefully consider my presentation and opted for casual/smart dress and did not display any badges or pendants that could reveal any religious denomination or political affiliation, or anything else that could indicate a values statement. The only 'badge' on display was my ID lanyard, giving my name and occupation. I selected this 'neutral' option in part because I knew I would be involved in offering a service to a diverse range of people and did not want to advertise membership of a group, or that I possessed values that may be contrary to those I was serving. I did not assume that doing so would create a barrier conflict or controversy to those who were not like-minded; it was more to do with knowing why I was there, which was to provide a social work service to anyone who was referred to it or requested it. Representatives from a variety of faiths visited the wards, such as Catholic priests, Anglican vicars and Muslim and Jewish clerics, dressed in apparel that identified them as such. This, of course, was appropriate as they were there to offer support to patients according to their respective faiths. This was quite different from the universality of what I was there to offer. I held other social work posts in other services during my career and always adopted this neutral presentation throughout.

NMC Standards

The Nursing & Midwifery Council has published a Code of Professional Standards of Practice and Behaviour for Nurses, Midwives and Nursing Associates that registered nurses, midwives and nursing associates must abide by. It is structured around four themes:

1. Prioritise people (contains five subheadings).
2. Practise effectively (contains seven subheadings).
3. Preserve safety (contains seven subheadings).
4. Promote professionalism and trust (contains six subheadings).

Each theme contains several subheadings, which are further broken down into a number of elements. For example, theme 1 has five subheadings:

1. *Treat people as individuals and uphold their dignity.*
2. *Listen to people and respond to their preferences and concerns.*
3. *Make sure that people's physical, social and psychological needs are assessed and responded to.*
4. *Act in the best interests of people at all times.*
5. *Respect people's right to privacy and confidentiality.*

The elements, for example from the first subheading from theme 1, treat people as individuals and uphold their dignity. To achieve this, you must:

1.1   Treat people with kindness, respect and compassion.
1.2   Make sure you deliver the fundamentals of care effectively.
1.3   Avoid making assumptions and recognise diversity and individual choice.
1.4   Make sure that any treatment, assistance or care for which you are responsible is delivered without undue delay.
1.5   Respect and uphold people's human rights.

(Nursing & Midwifery Council, 2024)

It adds an explanatory footnote to element 1.2:

The fundaments of care include, but are not limited to, nutrition, hydration, bladder and bowel care, physical handling and making sure that those receiving care are kept in clean and hygienic conditions. It includes making sure that those receiving care have adequate access to nutrition and hydration and making sure that you provide help to those who are not able to feed themselves or drink fluid unaided.

(Nursing & Midwifery Council, 2024)

It is worth noting that the explanatory note for element 1.2 was likely to have been added in response to the Mid Staffordshire Hospital scandal (see Introduction), where there was evidence of a collective failure to comply with this element.

In addition to the code for registrants, the Nursing & Midwifery Council also produces a Code of Professional Standards of Practice and Behaviour for student nurses, midwives and nursing associates with which those studying to become qualified in these occupations must comply.

The General Medical Council (GMC) is the regulatory body responsible for medical doctors in the United Kingdom. It has a code of conduct that all registrant members, in performing their duties must uphold. There are seven principles, first identified by the Nolan Committee in its report on standards in public life in May 1995 (Nolan Committee, 1995) and updated by the Committee on Standards in Public Life (2013):

1. *Selflessness.* Holders of public office should act solely in terms of the public interest.

2. *Integrity.* Holders of public office must not place themselves under any obligation to people or organisations that might try to inappropriately influence them in their work. They should not act or take decisions to gain financial or other material benefits for themselves, their family or their friends. They must declare and resolve any interests and relationships.

3. *Objectivity.* Holders of public office must act and take decisions impartially, fairly and on merit, using the best evidence and without discrimination or bias.

4. *Accountability.* Holders of public office are accountable for their decisions and actions, and must submit themselves to the scrutiny necessary to ensure this accountability.

5. *Openness.* Holders of public office should act and take decisions in an open and transparent manner. Information should not be withheld from the public unless there are clear and lawful reasons for so doing.

6. *Honesty.* Holders of public office should be truthful.

7. *Leadership.* Holders of public office should exhibit these principles in their own behaviour. They should actively promote and robustly support the principles and be willing to challenge poor behaviour wherever it occurs.

It is worth considering Principle 2 in a little more detail, particularly the duty to be alert to and avoid or declare any conflicts of interest. There may be specific circumstances pertinent to doctors who enjoy the hospitality of events funded by drug companies wishing to promote their products. Attending doctors have a responsibility to guard against their prescribing decisions to be unduly influenced by association.

There are, however, other conflicts of interests, or potential conflicts of interest, that a much wider range of employees need to be aware of and act upon. This is where an employee commences a personal relationship or is considering commencing a personal relationship with a colleague or, even more significantly, a client of a service for which they work. The safest way to deal with this is at the point of considering entering a personal relationship. It is important to seek out the policy statement of the employer regarding such matters and comply with it, including declaring it to the employee's supervisor or line manager if required to do so. It may be appropriate for the employee to cease to be the clinician providing the service to the client directly, as this could be deferred to a colleague. It is difficult to be prescriptive here as different situations may require different responses, but the important thing is for the employee to take appropriate action to safeguard themselves and the member of the public concerned against a conflict of interest charge, resulting in an accusation or actual some form of nepotism, preferential treatment or regard.

Some occupations, such as teaching, hold the teacher to be in a position of trust whereby it is absolutely inappropriate for them to enter into a personal relationship with a pupil, even if the pupil is over the age of consent. Such situations are considered abusive in nature, even where those involved do not consider them to be so. The same is true of other occupations, especially where the service user is considered vulnerable and there is a differential in power between the service user and the person providing the service.

Conclusion

This chapter has introduced a variety of pertinent issues around the topic of values, ethics and rights for health and social care practitioners. It has given examples of occupational standards and codes of conduct for some of the occupations within health and social care, and for the nursing profession and medical doctors. These were intended to provide a snapshot of the kind of principles such codes of practice entail, and are no substitute for a student's or practitioner's need to become familiar with the standards and codes of conduct appropriate to their occupation and to adopt them as the bedrock of their practice.

The central objective of this opening chapter was to set out why becoming familiar with the codes and standards for your occupation and abiding by them are essential for the practitioner. I hope to have succeeded in this objective, but if you remain in any doubt, then imagine the practitioner who isn't familiar with such requirements as a student in placement, or a practitioner who has read them but failed to abide by them in practice or has only a sketchy impression of what they entail. Not only is such a student at risk of failing their course, or such a practitioner at risk of failing to be registered as such or renew their registration, but anything they might do could pass for practice. If what they do is not informed by the professional standards defined for their occupation, anything goes – as we saw in the Winterbourne View case discussed in the Introduction.

Chapter 2 | Values: who and what do you stand up for?

Introduction

The values that interest us are intrinsic to each individual; these do not include simple preferences – for example, our choice of clothes or what we find useful. There are a couple of ways in which we can gain insights into the values we possess. In asking 'who' you stand up for, I am really asking who do you respect, admire, seek to emulate and aspire to be in some ways. If you then examine the qualities you think this person has, you will identify the characteristics you value. In considering what you stand up for, imagine you are in a large hall, around the walls of which are posters with value statements on them. For example, one poster states 'I support universal human rights.' Imagine many more values statements – which would you gather under if asked to stand by the ones that best represented you? They are the basis of how we behave and how we think others ought to behave.

In his article 'Holding onto Our Values', Neil Thompson (2020), rejects the idea that values are abstract concepts, describing them as 'very real, very concrete and very significant'. He asserts that they influence our thoughts, feelings, actions and reactions, and ultimately our effectiveness in achieving the outcomes to which we aspire.

In exploring our values, it may be helpful to consider a definition. Values are defined as *'One's principles or standards; one's judgement of what is valuable or important in life'* (Thompson, 1995).

This definition implies that values are held individually, that our 'personal set' is unique to us. This might be the case, but it is also true that they may be held in common with other people. This could be because those people are like-minded or have an interest in common. For example, a group of people who volunteer to work for the National Trust are likely to find that they hold values of appreciating history, heritage and nature in common. Or the members of a branch of the Liberal Democrat Party are likely to hold the values of liberty and democracy in common. There is a clear rationale in these two examples for why the individuals concerned would be likely to hold the values suggested in common, as they are enshrined in what the respective organisations stand for; this is probably what attracted their members to join them. But we cannot assume they hold values in common that are not directly relevant to the organisations they belong to – for example, we cannot assume that the National Trust volunteers all value liberty and democracy any more than we can assume that the members of the Liberal Democrat Party all value history, heritage and nature. With other, more disparate groups of people, it cannot be *assumed* that they hold any values in common. Sometimes, especially around the times of general elections and new administrations, the term 'values' is bandied about in an attempt to associate a set of values with a politician or brand of political thinking and attract voters as a result. For example, in 1993 the Conservative leader, John Major, campaigned on a platform advocating 'family values', extolling the virtues of 'back to basics'. However, when examined, slogans like these can appear vague regarding what precisely is meant by such terms. Again, in political discourse, the term 'British values' has been used to encompass such values as democracy, the rule of law, respect, tolerance and individual liberty, implying that all those who identify themselves as British hold these values in common. This is doubtful – for example, not all live by the rule of law for if we did our prisons would not be as full as they are. Those responsible for making such claims must guard against hypocrisy lest they undermine the veracity of such claims, and thus encourage cynicism. For example, later in John Major's campaign, his extra-marital affair with Edwina Curry exposed him to hypocrisy, given the assumption that 'family values' include fidelity. Furthermore, in the vote to leave the European Union in 2016, Scotland voted to remain but was forced to leave as part of the United Kingdom, which can hardly be said to be democratic.

We have already learned a few things about values. They are often described as abstract concepts, but their effect is very real, and they can be held individually or in common. It cannot be assumed that members of a particular group have the same set of values, but they may hold in common the values associated with that group. Those claiming or extolling the virtues of specific values also need to be seen to uphold them in their behaviour, lest they be accused of hypocrisy. It is a test sometimes referred to as 'walking the walk as well as talking the talk'.

Now let's think about values that would be appropriate for those working in health and social care. They perhaps would not be exclusive to health and social care, but would be applicable to all occupations that seek to offer caring, professional relationships with their clients, so might also include counselling and social work in addition to the occupations discussed in Chapter 1. A value that could be considered a prerequisite for all of these would be a desire help people. But which other values, in addition to this common denominator, do you think would be essential and desirable for members of such a workforce to hold?

Exercise

In the space below, list five values that you consider essential for those working in the caring professions to hold. It might assist you to imagine you are an admissions tutor for a place on the course to study your chosen occupation. What values would you be looking for in your applicants?

1.
2.
3.
4.
5.

And now see if you can identify five values you consider desirable for those working in the caring professions to hold.

1.
2.
3.
4.
5.

Below are some suggestions for responding to this exercise. I am not presenting my suggestions as the definitive 'right' answer, but rather offering something with which to compare your own.

Essential

- » The quality of other people's lives is important and matters to you.
- » There are standards below which the care and treatment of others should not fall.

- » You find having empathy and having compassion for others and their situations comes easily to you.
- » You think it important to hear the wishes and feelings of others.
- » Equality of opportunity and opposing prejudice and unlawful discrimination are values for which you stand up.

Desirable

- » You value diversity in relation to people's ethnicity, gender, disability, religion and sexuality.
- » Being aware of your own needs and addressing them is important to you, and you seek support as appropriate.
- » You enjoy goal-setting for yourself and acquiring new skills and knowledge.
- » You acknowledge the benefits that can come from group and teamwork, and the contribution you can make.
- » You regard having access to information about people as a privilege and understand the need for confidentiality and circumstances where breaching this is required.

I stress that this is not a definitive list; these are simply the values I would be looking for in my applicants were I the admissions tutor for a health and social care course. How did your list compare with mine?

Exercise

- » Undertake an audit comparing the values you identified as essential and desirable with values you currently possess.
- » Then undertake an audit of the values I identified as essential and desirable. Are there values that you possess or want to acquire?

Outcomes

It may be that you are completely satisfied with 'where you are' in respect of your values, but it is also possible that these lists provided some 'food for thought' regarding the extent to which your values currently mirror those in the list. Also significant is where you are in progressing towards qualification in your chosen occupation or your experience if newly qualified. I would expect any programme of qualification in the professions identified in Chapter 1 to include learning that would hone and develop the values you held at the outset and those acquired as you progressed towards qualification and registration. In any event, it is always worth 'taking stock' of your values periodically, to see how they are bearing up to the experience of placements and practice, and as part of maintaining your own health and well-being. There is absolutely nothing wrong with the practitioner who finds themselves revisiting their reasons for why they do their job; indeed, this is preferable to the practitioner who loses sight of knowing why they do the job they do.

Where do we get our values from?

Social learning theory tells us that we acquire behaviours by observing those modelled or demonstrated to us and copying them. So we could go back to our early infancy to find the origins of our exposure to the behaviour and the values that underpinned it – the values of our parents and significant others within our family. Indeed, this influence can be profound, and it is often the mechanism by which values are internalised and transmitted from one generation to the next. However, it is not the sole source of exposure to values. As we grow, so does our social world as we experience nursery and school, acquire friends and engage in activities outside the family. In our teenage years, the potency of parental influence tends to lessen, as the influence of peers and social media increases. Selecting values purely from those we see others exhibiting is not the only way we accrue our own. We may choose to adopt them or change the values we have, due to a specific experience we've had or something we've learned about through education.

A significant source of influence on our values is the culture we are born into and in which we grow up. Differences in culture provide a rich vein of diversity in human life and are themselves influenced by a sense of national identity, ethnicity and religion to greater or lesser extents. In some countries, religion is amalgamated into culture and the legal framework. Here, the societal values will reflect those of the dominant religion, for example, in Jewish communities or Islamic countries. Banks (2012, p 9) states that most researchers agree that societies where religion dominates cultural values include the following features:

» convictions about what is most important in life (experiences such as birth, death, sex and sorrow);
» rituals;
» beliefs about existence (and what happens when you die);
» codes of conduct;

- » communal life;
- » experiences of transcendence (enlightenment, redemption, etc).

Banks goes onto say that these features of religion can be disputed and manifest with different meanings in different countries.

Duncan (2010, p 22) argues that the development of our own values is more complicated than just absorbing those of our family and quotes Tones and Green (2004), saying that our values are the result of *'the interplay between individual personality and the culture, institutions, and society in which that personality dwells'*. However, it is worth considering the extent to which this 'interplay' is a product of indoctrination in our formative years or the product of freely chosen values based on what we have decided to hold dear and what is important to us when mature. Of course, our values may consist of a mix of these two.

Personal and professional values

So far in this chapter, we have primarily considered personal values, although we have examined what values you think would be essential or desirable for those wanting to work in the caring professions, some of which overlap the distinction between personal and professional values. We might, however, differentiate these: personal values are what we, as autonomous individuals choose to regard as ethically relevant, worth owning and standing up for, whereas professional values are what we, as professionals, are obliged to adopt and apply in the course of our work. They will usually involve observance of a code of practice.

The attributes of those holding professional values could include:

- » being knowledgeable;
- » being competent;
- » possessing good interpersonal skills;
- » being trustworthy;
- » having integrity;
- » being reliable.

And they would be ethically committed to:

- » service provision;
- » person-centred practice;
- » client self-determination;
- » non-discriminatory, lawful practice;

» human rights;
» social justice;
» a code of practice and practice standards.

The requirement to uphold professional values is non-negotiable, and their application must be exercised in an even-handed and equitable manner, whoever our client or patient might be. The practitioner cannot discriminate or speculate on who may be considered by the layperson to be more or less deserving of treatment or care.

However, there will be situations that test this. For example, among those waiting to be seen in the urgent care centre of your local hospital are a frail elderly woman who has a head injury after a fall and a young woman who has self-harmed by cutting her arms. It is not the first time she has presented as needing treatment for this. Both need the practitioner's clinical skills, care and compassion.

A more extreme example could test this further still. The riots in Dublin that took place on 23 November 2023 were allegedly prompted by a knife attack on five people, including three children and a woman in her thirties who had tried to defend the children. One of the children, who was five, and the woman were critically injured. All five, including the perpetrator of the attack, were taken to hospital for treatment. All five need the clinician's skill, care and compassion. Any consideration of retribution for the attacker must be left for the criminal justice system.

Differences between personal and professional values

There may be some differences between your personal values and the professional values of your chosen occupation, but they should not be significant. Ideally, they should be a good match and reflect the essence of the two sets. A good match would mean they were congruent, enabling the practitioner to be authentic – meaning true to their own personal values – rather than having to manage a pretence to uphold professional values they do not hold at a personal level. Such a 'lack of fit', or incongruence, could result in what psychologist Leon Festinger (1957) termed cognitive dissonance. This occurs when someone holds two or more attitudes or beliefs simultaneously that are inconsistent or even contradictory. This results in psychological tension that, if confronted, makes us feel uncomfortable. We tend to seek to lessen this discomfort or dissonance through a variety of justifications, but these rarely stand up to close examination and often appear hypocritical.

Of course, few of us could claim that we do not exhibit some degree of hypocrisy in our purported views when compared with our behaviour. For example, I value the idea of animal welfare but enjoy eating chicken and avoid serious consideration of modern chicken-rearing practices for the food industry. I could address this in part by ensuring that I only consumed corn-fed, free-range poultry, but I do not insist on this. On occasion, many of us might admit to a little over-indulgence with alcohol or food, and some of us still smoke but we tend to dismiss or minimise the risks to our own health in maintaining these habits.

We might forgive ourselves for such foibles and say they are part of life, but the implications for significant dissonance between personal and professional values are of a different magnitude and have consequences not only for ourselves in terms of stress, dissatisfaction in our work and potential burnout, but also for our clients, who may receive a lesser quality of service as a result. Imagine a scenario in which a young, single Muslim female presents herself to her local GP surgery seeking to discuss her options for an unwanted pregnancy. She thinks she is about 12 weeks pregnant and does not want to be a mother and rear a child at this time in her life. The nurse practitioner she sees supports the pro-life movement and holds sincere beliefs about abortion not only resulting in the death of the baby but also being detrimental to the well-being of the mother, irrespective of her personal circumstances. This proposed consultation causes the nurse practitioner an ethical dilemma because there are significant differences between her personal values and her professional values that oblige her to include the option of abortion up to 24 weeks, presented in a neutral manner, free of her personal values. If she failed to do this due to being true to her personal values, by only discussing adoption as an option, she would be failing in her duty to provide the best service she could to her service user.

While it is a valid perspective to disagree with the current lawful position of a woman's right to choose to keep a baby, relinquish it for adoption or abort the foetus, it would be wise for someone with such a view to avoid an occupation or a role within an occupation that would present the practitioner with such a dilemma. A practitioner might be in sympathy with those who would like the law changed to allow voluntary euthanasia in the United Kingdom. However, if they worked in palliative care, their personal view would not present an ethical dilemma provided they understood that they must support the current legal position, so if a patient for whom they were caring asked for information or help with assisted dying, they should decline and would need to explain that doing so would be illegal and against current medical ethics (see Chapter 4). If the practitioner held a radical view on euthanasia and fervently believed that people should have the right to end their lives in a manner and at a time of their choosing, working in palliative care would be an unwise career choice.

Do you hold any personal values that have the potential to create dissonance with your professional values that could present you with an ethical dilemma? If so, how could this best be managed? An honest discussion within clinical supervision would be an appropriate way forward. For example, the nurse practitioner in the above scenario might be tempted to keep quiet about her pro-life stance; she could tell herself that, as the client is a Muslim, she will be opposed to having an abortion anyway due to her religion, so she could avoid raising and discussing this option without depriving her of choice. This would be doing a professional disservice to her client, as she is making this assumption to avoid compromising her own personal values rather than giving her client the information she needs to make an informed decision. The professional way to address this problem would be for her to disclose her pro-life stance in supervision and the dilemma avoided through such referrals being directed to alternative practitioners.

A potential issue for health and social care practitioners concerns the mixed economy of service provision, as alluded to in the Introduction. In August 2023, there were 7,745,030 patients waiting for consultant-led referral to treatment. Nearly 3,250,000 of these had been waiting for over 18 weeks, 397,000 of which had been waiting for over a year – 321 times as many as in August 2019 before the pandemic. However, a backlog of patients is not a new phenomenon, as over four million were waiting for treatment in August 2007 (British Medical Association, 2024). The pandemic has been a significant factor in the recent increase, but at the time of writing, the current industrial action is also having an impact on the numbers, which continue to rise.

A founding principle of the NHS is free access at the point of clinical need, but the backlog in the numbers of those awaiting treatment is creating significant delays in the procedures being undertaken, extending the time for which any pain and discomfort must be endured. It is possible to avoid such delays by paying for treatment from private health providers, who make an important contribution to the mixed economy of health care in the United Kingdom. I do not intend to make any point about the morality of public versus private health care provision or comment on those who can afford to pay and fast-track access to treatment. But it is important that health and social care practitioners are at ease with whichever system they are working in. If access to treatment free at the point of need is an important principle to you, working within the NHS is likely to offer a better 'fit' with your personal values.

The behaviour of patients and anyone seeking medical treatment

Members of the public seeking medical treatment are not obliged to apply the same professional standards and codes of conduct that practitioners are, and sadly many of those who provide health and care services have been subject to verbally or physically abusive behaviour.

An NHS staff survey held in 2022 reported that of those who completed it, 27.8 per cent had experienced an incident of harassment, bullying or verbal abuse from patients, service users, relatives or other members of the public in the last 12 months. In the same survey, 14.7 per cent claimed to have experienced at least one incident of physical violence from patients, service users, relatives or other members of the public in the same period (NHS, 2023).

Such events should not occur, and they should attract censure, which could extend to a refusal of treatment or, in very serious cases, prosecution. It is difficult to be prescriptive about such instances as some may be the result of diminished responsibility through mental illness, or alcohol or substance misuse. However, some may be due to discrimination, contravening the *Equality Act 2010*, meriting challenge. Other situations may simply be expressing a preference, such as wishing to be admitted to a same-sex ward, the reasonableness of which needs to be judged using professional judgement, and the availability of same-sex ward beds. Some situations may be the result of increased stress due to extended waiting times or delayed or cancelled procedures, reactions to which may be nullified through the practitioner's good interpersonal skills and empathetic response. Although members of the public do not have the same high bar of professional standards and codes of conduct that practitioners must comply with, this does not mean they can act with impunity in response to everyday frustrations. They are bound by the common expectations of civility and reasonableness to which we are all subject. Sadly, it is commonplace to see notices reminding us of this, stating that service providers are exercising a 'zero tolerance' approach to any expression of abuse toward their staff. The implications of such notices can be balanced, if not offset, by the cards and notes of thanks and appreciation for the care and treatment patients have received that often adorn noticeboards in health and social care waiting areas and hospital wards.

Codes of conduct, standards and behaviour in health and social care occupations

The regulatory bodies for many occupations within health and social care produce standards of competence as part of their duties, some of which were introduced in Chapter 1; however, they are also responsible for setting out codes of conduct, behaviour and ethics for their registered practitioners. Sometimes these are amalgamated, sometimes they remain separate. For our purposes here, ethics can be thought of as the formal expression of professional values. (Ethics is the topic of Chapters 3 and 4, and will be discussed in detail there.) Some examples of these codes are listed below.

- » The NMC produces Professional Standards of Practice and Behaviour for Nurses, Midwives and Nursing Associates, known as 'The Code'.
- » The GMC produces Codes of Conduct for council members.
- » The HCPC produces Standards of Conduct, Performance and Ethics for registrants for all the professions over which it has regulatory responsibility. It also publishes guidance on conduct and ethics for students studying for qualification in those professions.
- » The Royal Pharmaceutical Society produces Professional Standards and Guidelines for pharmacists.
- » The General Dental Council produces Standards of Conduct, Performance and Ethics that govern dental professionals.
- » The General Optical Council produces Standards of Practice for optometrists and dispensing opticians.
- » The General Osteopathic Council produces Standards of Practice and Guidance for osteopaths.
- » The General Chiropractic Council produces Standards of Conduct, Performance and Ethics for chiropractors in addition to their Code of Practice and Standards of Proficiency.
- » The British Association of Social Workers (BASW) produces a Code of Ethics for Social Workers.

It is, of course, compulsory for registrants of the occupations listed above (including the 15 for which the HCPC is responsible) to both be familiar and comply with the standards of performance and codes of conduct that govern their profession. It is advisable for those studying for qualifications in those professions to be aware of the standards and codes of conduct of the profession they are seeking to join, as well as being familiar, and complying, with their course requirements regarding conduct and ethics as student and while on practice placements.

Professional boundaries

One of the skills health and social care practitioners need to develop is knowing when, what and how best to impose professional boundaries as necessary. There may be situations where some flexibility would be appropriate in accordance with how 'tight' or 'loose' the practitioner is in their comfort with the application of professional boundaries, but there are other situations where an appropriate response is not so nuanced and where policy and codes of conduct and behaviour need to strictly adhered to.

Exercise

Boundaries

Consider the following scenarios.

Scenario 1

You are an occupational therapist undertaking a home assessment visit to a new client to assess his mobility following a slight stroke. He answers the door dressed only in a towel around his waist and had apparently just got out of the shower. Do you:

  a) Follow him in, presuming he will go and get dressed?

  b) Ask him to get dressed while you wait outside?

  c) Suggest you rearrange the appointment?

Option (b) may be the most appropriate here. You do not know this client and your assessment does not include any sort of examination. Rearranging the appointment would mean visiting again, so would not be the best use of your time – although, in addition to option (b), you might ask whether it is convenient to go ahead with the appointment when he has dressed.

Scenario 2

You are a Macmillan nurse who cared for your patient for three years, prior to her recent death. Caring for patients suffering from cancer is your job and you have cared for many whose condition was terminal, who have died. There was something about this particular patient, though, and you were touched by the loss and will miss visiting her. Importantly, she did not receive 'special' treatment or care from you – nothing you would not have done for any other of your patients while you were caring for them; however, on this occasion, you would like to attend her funeral to pay your respects. Do you:

  a) Ignore this feeling, thinking attending would be unprofessional?

  b) Speak with the family, who you know, and ask whether you may attend?

  c) Choose option (b) but run it by your clinical supervisor?

Option (c) may be the most appropriate here. It is important to listen to your feelings as part of your well-being, and paying your respects would attend to these feelings. The bereaved family members are likely to be very pleased about your wish and feel it confirms the regard in which you held your patient.

Scenario 3

You are a physiotherapist undertaking an assessment of a client at your clinic. In your bag is a copy of a book your book club is currently reading. Your client notices this and says the author is one of his favourites, but adds that he has not read that particular book. Do you:

- a) Agree that the author is a very good writer of that particular genre and proceed with your assessment?
- b) Discuss the author's work in general and inquire which books your client has read?
- c) Offer to lend your client the book?

Option (a) may be the most appropriate here. The purpose of the consultation was to undertake an assessment of joint articulation and, while it is appropriate to acknowledge his observation of your reading, developing the conversation into the author's work is not.

Scenario 4

You are a bereavement counsellor and seeing a client for the first time. The client has lost a partner after many years together. He found it difficult to talk about their life together initially but became engaged in the later part of the one-hour session. The conversation has reached a significant point when you really need to draw the session to a close as the last appointment of your day is waiting. The client wants to continue. Do you:

- a) Get round it by saying you will extend the session by 20 minutes and ask your next client to wait?
- b) Say you have another client to see, but could meet the client in the pub round the corner in an hour's time?
- c) Empathetically acknowledge that you have reached a significant point in the story of your client's relationship with his partner, but say you need to end this session now and you will pick it up from where you left off at next week's appointment.

Option (c) is most appropriate here. Keeping your next client waiting is unethical and (b) is quite inappropriate. It is not advisable to run over fixed appointment times in this kind of service.

Scenario 5

You are a trainee social worker on your final placement co-working a case with a qualified social worker. A child has had to be placed with foster parents due to the significant and persistence substance misuse issues of the birth parents. You are visiting the birth parents to discuss supervised contact with their child. You explain that one of the foster carers, either Ms X or Ms Y, will bring the child to the contact centre at the appointed date and time. The father expresses concern that his child has been placed with a same-sex couple and makes derogatory comments about lesbians. You have a partner of the same sex and find his comments offensive. Do you:

a) Disclose the fact that you have a partner of the same sex and say you find his comments offensive?

b) Ignore his comments and move the conversation onto the child's schooling?

c) Politely challenge his comments, saying they are unacceptable as it is unlawful to discriminate against people on the grounds of their sexual orientation and cite the *Equality Act 2010*.

Option (c) is most appropriate here. Failing to challenge his oppressive comments (option (b)) is unprofessional. Option (a) involves disclosure of personal information and is not advisable in this situation (see concluding comments).

Scenario 6

You are a newly qualified junior doctor working in the emergency department of a local hospital. You are of small stature and have a youthful appearance. You see your next patient, who has been waiting over four hours, and comments on 'finally' being called into your consultation room. Once inside, he looks at you and says, 'You don't look old enough to be a doctor – do you know what you are doing?' Do you:

a) Become flustered by his ageist and rude comment and suggest he return to the waiting area and wait to be seen by a colleague?

b) Brush aside his comments and ask how you may help?

c) Admit that you are fortunate enough to have a youthful appearance but assert that you have undertaken all the training and qualifications to be a junior doctor and ask what appears to be his problem?

Again, option (c) is the most appropriate response here, as his ageist comments should be challenged, although you might concede that you appear youthful. It would be unethical to ignore the question and wrong to give any credence to his rudeness with option (a), as while you might not prefer to treat this patient, any reluctance needs to be overcome.

Scenario 7

You are a podiatrist visiting a woman with limited mobility. After you have treated her feet, she invites you to share a cup of tea. While you consider this, she adds 'But I haven't got any milk' and asks if you'd be a love and pop out to the corner shop to buy some. Do you:

a) Thank her but decline the tea, adding that you need to go onto your next appointment?

b) Thank her, accept the tea but say you are happy to have it without milk?

c) Agree to pop out to the corner shop to purchase a pint of milk with the money she gave you?

There is nothing significantly wrong with any of these options. You may come across situations during home visits where your client has run out of something, including foodstuffs. If there are mobility or transport problems, you may be tempted to go the extra mile and fetch the item, but this needs to be restricted to 'one offs' and not become routine as this is not what you are there for. If requests persist, alternative solutions need to be found.

Scenario 8

You are a nurse on a respiratory ward in a local hospital. You have nursed a patient with aggravated Covid-19 symptoms for four months and happily your patient is now well enough to be discharged. Your patient returned to the ward with a gift for you to express his gratitude for the care he had received. You open the gift to find an expensive item of personalised jewellery. Do you:

a) Graciously accept the gift but keep it secret from your colleagues on the ward?

b) Thank your patient for the gift but say you must consult the hospital's policy on receiving gifts from patients or discuss with your clinical supervisor before you are able to decide whether you can accept it?

c) Thank your patient but say you must decline the gift.

Option (b) could be the most sensitive option here although following consultation, option (c) may need to be taken. A box of chocolates for the ward staff is one thing but something expensive and personalised merits further consideration. Most organisations within the caring professions have policy statements on staff receiving gifts from their service users and it is always advisable to abide by the policy, which may result in option (c) in this example. The Nursing and Midwifery Council's (2024) Code of Professional Conduct, clause 7.4 states *'You must refuse any gift, favour or hospitality that might be interpreted, now or in the future, as an attempt to obtain preferential consideration'* (Caulfield, 2005, p 165). This implies that the gift is not the primary issue, but the way you accept it may be construed poorly by others, now or at some time in the future, including after the clinical relationship has ended.

Scenario 9

You are a community care officer visiting a client at their home to undertake a review of her care needs. You have arranged the appointment, but your client does not appear to be at home. You are a little early so you wait a few minutes in the front garden. You look down the hill to see whether you can see your client coming home and, sure enough, you see her walking up the hill, unaided by the walking sticks she is carrying with her. She is not aware that you have seen her and when she sees you she immediately starts using her sticks and appears to have some restriction of mobility. Do you:

a) Not mention that you saw her walking unaided and proceed with the review as planned?

b) Not mention that you saw her walking unaided and proceed with the review as planned but, as she claims to suffer from restricted mobility, discuss this apparent deception with your supervisor upon returning to the office?

c) Address what you saw with your client and politely inquire about when and how the apparent improvement in her mobility occurred?

Option (c) is appropriate here, although option (b) can also be considered, provided it results in the difference in what the client appears to be able to do compared with what she claims she can do, as this could involve benefit fraud. Option (a) is unprofessional as it involves collusion with a likely deception.

Scenario 10

You are a physiotherapist working in a rehabilitation unit. You have been working with a patient who has had a lower leg amputation after an injury while serving in the army. He is nearing the end of his treatment and tells you he likes you and asks you for a date. In other circumstances, you might consider this but given the context in which you have known him, the suggestion feels a little strange. Do you:

a) Thank him for the offer and say you feel flattered but must decline as you already have a boyfriend?

b) Thank him for the offer and accept?

c) Thank him for the offer and agree to meet for a drink, but only after he has been discharged from the rehabilitation service's care?

Considering entering a personal relationship was discussed in Chapter 1, and staff are usually advised to avoid this – certainly while the professional relationship continues. A view could be taken that it is inappropriate at any time, but a more liberal interpretation could allow this, so if the physiotherapist was interested in taking up the offer, option (c) could be appropriate. It would be advisable to seek policy guidance on this before any decision was made.

It is difficult to write an exercise that could offer an opinion on the many varied circumstances that call for the imposition of boundaries and to offer guidance on how rigidly or loosely it would be appropriate to apply them. Often it will be down to professional judgement unless prescribed by policy and procedure, as is likely to be the case when engaging in personal relationships or receiving gifts from clients, which may not be the only circumstances governed by policy. There are, however, some basic principles which it may be wise to adopt.

» In going that 'extra mile' for your client be aware of how your behaviour may construed by your client. It is fine for them to think you are kind and helpful but undesirable if they conclude it is because they are special to you or are in receipt of special treatment that would not be available to other clients.

» There can be occasions where some disclosure of personal information would be appropriate and helpful to your client, but check that your decision to share is motivated by this and has not arisen from a need within yourself.

» Avoid colluding with something that you know to be wrong through fear of confrontation. Good interpersonal skills can help you manage challenge in a way that is assertive rather than aggressive or confrontational.

» Not all situations will require an instant response. If you are in doubt about how best to proceed or respond to a situation, you may be able to defer until you can consult a colleague, your supervisor or manager, or your organisation's manual on policy and procedure.

Conclusion

This chapter has considered values from several standpoints. Initially, it explored what is meant by the term 'values' and what started out as an amorphous idea took shape and form through the ownership of the values we possess. Some discussion took place as to where we get out values from. It then went onto identify the values we considered essential and desirable in a health and social care practitioner. Personal and professional values were discussed together with the need to ideally keep significant differences between these to a minimum. Examples were given of codes of conduct and standards of behaviour produced by the regulatory bodies of some of the professions within health and social care, which set out the broad expectations of registrants. Finally, we considered some scenarios that presented the practitioner with options for what would be the most appropriate response to be accommodating yet establish and maintain professional boundaries.

Chapter 3 | Ethics: where do we get our sense of 'what is right'?

Introduction

What does the term 'ethics' mean? Ethics refers to the body of knowledge concerned with moral principles. It does not have an exact definition, but included within its overall meaning are the concepts of a formal expression of values; bodies of ideas that deal with morality and distinguish between right and wrong; and a set of moral principles such as professional standards, to which practitioners in health and social care are committed. Different ideas about ethics can be represented in different 'schools' or traditions explored in moral philosophy.

We may or may not be aware of which of these ethical schools or traditions we choose to guide our decision-making, but we do rely on them for our sense of what is right or wrong. However, there is no universal consensus on what is right and what is wrong. Our view is largely dictated by which of these schools or traditions we choose to inform our sense of what is right or wrong. This chapter will introduce some of the mainstream schools or traditions in moral philosophy and will explore how different outcomes in what is considered right or wrong result from the same problem being applied to different schools. The following schools or traditions will be considered: Kantian ethics, utilitarian ethics, existential and humanistic ethics, modernism, radical ethics, observance of a higher authority through faith – for example, natural law – and, finally, postmodernism.

Mainstream ethical schools or traditions of moral philosophy

Kantian or deontic ethics: action rooted in duty

This school of ethics originates for the work of the German philosopher Immanuel Kant (1724–1804). Important works in his ideas in moral philosophy include *Critique of Pure Reason* (1781), *Critique of Practical Reason* (1788) and *Groundwork of the Metaphysic of Morals* (1792). In Kant's view, it is the human ability to reason and to act rationally that marks us out from other species and makes us what we are (Wood, 2008). In Kantian ethical philosophy, an act only has moral worth if the motive for doing it is through duty, a duty owed to a service user or a concept. The act should be underpinned by a principle. Another important criterion of Kantian ethics is that what is right for one person is also right for everyone else; ethics should be 'universalisable', meaning they can be applied universally. For example, it would be 'right' that human rights were afforded to all human beings, not just to those humans in a particular society or part of the world. Kant rejects the idea that outcomes contribute to the moral worth of an act; the only motive necessary is the sense of duty, rule or principle, regardless of inclination, self-interest or consequence. He developed the idea of a 'categorical imperative', which he explained in his own words as *'I ought never to act except in such a way that I can also will that my maxim should become a universal law'* (Kant, 2016, p 96). This means that, in considering whether the act or action you are proposing to carry out or the concept you are advocating is ethically moral, you need to ask yourself whether it would be a good idea if it were applied to the whole world as a universal rule or law. If it would, then it is ethically moral.

So, let's apply Kantian ethics to the question of how we should regard other people. Kant would say we should respect other human beings simply because they are human beings. We should not respect other people because we like or admire them or find them attractive, or because we need something they have. His categorical imperative does not mean one size fits all and it does not mean we are all the same, but it does mean that what is good for some people, such as having sufficient food or access to goods and services, is likely to be good for all people collectively. Another example of a categorical imperative is to tell the truth. In our dealings with others, we usually assume that they are telling the truth; the world would not work if, at random, half of us lied. Yet there are circumstances where, on occasion, we find it convenient to be less than truthful, or deliberately lie – for example, telling our children about Santa Claus and the Tooth Fairy. Kant would be critical of this playing fast and loose with the truth; his maxim would be to always tell the truth, irrespective of the consequences.

Kant also thought it right to only *'act in a way that you always treat humanity, never simply as a means but always at the same time as an end'* (Kant, 2016, p 91). In other words, never treat people to get something else but always with their full humanity in mind, as an end in itself and not to achieve some other objective. For example, Huntington's Chorea is a fatal neurological disease, genetically transmitted, in which its sufferer's nervous system gradually disintegrates. It is a very distressing illness and undoubtedly the world would be better off without it. But how might we rid the world of it? One way would be to identify all its sufferers and carriers of the gene responsible for it and forcibly sterilise them. Within a generation, we would rid the world of this disease. There may be some people who would not mind being sterilised, but not all would agree and would think the practice barbarous if imposed against their will. The means applied to achieve this outcome would contravene Kantian ethics by denying people having children; it would be treating them as a means to achieve an end: the eradication of Huntington's Chorea.

If you have gathered that Kant sets the bar very high in terms of his expectations for human behaviour, you are quite correct. In fact, critics of his ideas ask what counts as a universal judgement and whether we can all be bound by it. Some consider his expectations overly rigid and inflexible. However, he makes an invaluable contribution to practitioners within health and social care, which will be explained at the end of Chapter 4.

> ### Applications of principles derived from Kantian ethics
>
> These include duty to a code of practice, respect for persons and their individual wishes and feelings, confidentiality, acceptance and non-judgementalism.

Utilitarianism: a philosophy of utility

At its simplest, this school of ethical philosophy involves the promotion of happiness. It is characterised by the *consequentialist principle*, which states that the rightness or wrongness of an action or concept is determined by the outcome, result or consequence of that action or concept. If the outcome, result or consequence produced happiness and satisfaction for the majority, it is a good and ethically 'right' action. It does not matter whether the outcome is unfavourable for a minority; it is the view of the majority that counts. Of particular influence in the ideas of utilitarian ethics is the philosopher Jeremy Bentham (1748–1832). He developed these ideas in his book *Introduction to the Principles of Morals and Legislation*, first published in 1789. He said that '*nature has placed mankind under the governance of two sovereign masters, pain and pleasure*' (Bentham, 2007, p 11). He went on to say that '*an action then may be said to be conformable to the principle of utility when the tendency it has to augment the happiness of the community is greater than any it has to diminish it*' (Bentham, 2007, p 127). The Victorian thinker John Stuart Mill (1803–1873) built on Bentham's work in his publications *On Liberty* (Mill, 1859) and *Utilitarianism* (Mill, 2014). Mill's ethics is egalitarian and impartial in that the identity of the individual is irrelevant, as each individual holds equal moral weight regarding whether an action has produced overall benefit for the majority. Utilitarianism does not concern itself with the motive behind an action, only the outcome, which must be about producing the greatest happiness for the greatest number of people.

One obvious application of utilitarianism is our democratic voting system. The result of the 2016 Brexit referendum on whether the United Kingdom should leave or remain a member of the European Union was 52 per cent for leaving and 48 per cent for remaining, so we left as that was the wish of the majority. However, just because a majority think one way does not mean the minority will change their mind and fall in line with the view of the majority, as many of the 48 per cent undoubtedly continue to think the decision was wrong and not beneficial for the United Kingdom. The result also had an apparently undemocratic outcome for Scottish voters, 62 per cent of whom voted to remain but then had to leave as Scotland is part of the United Kingdom (Electoral Commission 2016). Another example of a utilitarian initiative is the addition of fluoride to the water supply to help combat tooth decay. Other examples can be seen in our everyday life. The government collects revenue through taxation to fund public services, the welfare state and pensions. Not all taxpayers use all these services or claim benefits or pensions, but they do not receive a refund for not doing so, which means those who wish to be taxed significantly less are a minority and those benefiting from such services are the majority. It could be argued that our parliamentary system is utilitarian in that a majority of voters elect the government, whose members pass laws by which we are governed.

Critics of utilitarianism cite several problems. There are issues with the measurement of happiness and who exactly makes up the majority. It is possible that an amoral motive could result in benefit for a majority. For example, in the United Kingdom it is considered, quite rightly, both immoral and illegal for adults to use the bodies of children for their own sexual gratification. However, if opinion on this question was sought solely from a group of sex offenders, a different outcome may be obtained that could conform to the principle of utility. In society generally, such a group would be in a minority, but if they were a remote tribe somewhere where such practices were dominant, it could normalise rather than criminalise such behaviour. This was a problem in St Kitts and Nevis. Should we also consider the immediate or short-term happiness or benefit an action brings, or look to its longer-term consequences. For example, the mining and burning of fossil fuels gave rise to the Industrial Revolution, which realised many benefits for numerous countries around the world; now, however, we face the consequences of global warming, which if unchecked poses a threat to humanity.

Applications of principles derived from utility

These include non-preferential treatment, the promotion of public health and the desire to uphold public trust and confidence in the social care professions.

ETHICS

A thought experiment to compare outcomes using Kantian and utilitarian ethics

Consider the photograph in Figure 3.1. It is of members of a boys' class in an Austrian school in 1901. Two of the boys are circled: one is Ludwig Wittgenstein, who was of Jewish heritage and became a famous linguistic philosopher; the other is Adolf Hitler, who achieved notoriety through instigating World War II and the Holocaust.

Figure 3.1 Fichier: Hitler at school (Adapted from Wikipedia: https://fr.m.wikipedia.org/wiki/Fichier:Hitler_at_school_in_1901.jpg)

Imagine if Wittgenstein, as a 12 year-old, could somehow know what his fellow classmate, Hitler, would become and that he would be responsible for the deaths of millions of people, and contemplated saving the world by killing him. Would such an act be ethical? If you asked someone applying Kantian ethics, the answer would be no, as killing a child could not be converted into an acceptable universal law or principle. However, if you asked someone applying utilitarian ethics, the answer would be undoubtedly yes, as a majority would consider it better to rid the world of this dictator-to-be.

The application of Kantian and utilitarian ethics in the workplace

You are a community care officer working for a local authority and have undertaken an assessment of need for an elderly person living in the community under the

49

provisions of the *Care Act 2014*. In an application of Kantian ethics, you have a duty to provide your client with the best service you can offer, and you have assessed your client's needs as requiring three home visits per day from home care workers: a morning visit to assist them with getting up, showering, toileting and breakfast; a lunchtime visit to prepare food; and an evening visit to prepare for bedtime. You set this out in your assessment report and send it to your manager.

Your manager is responsible for a budget to cover the home care costs of all those who are eligible for a service under the *Care Act 2014* in the area that the local authority serves. As such your manager's decision-making is guided by utilitarian principles. The manager is projected to overspend this budget and must make some savings to avoid this as they cannot run out of money and be in a position of being unable to offer any help to some of the people in the community for whom they are responsible.

You are not pleased with your manager's decision to allow only a morning and an evening visit to your client, despite your assessment. But once you have understood the different frameworks of ethics used by you and your manager, the difference in where you are coming from, which has resulted in different decisions, is understood. You also realise that while it is your duty to assess your client's needs to the best of your ability, you can also see your manager's responsibility to share the finite resources in their budget fairly between all those people in need in the area for which the local authority is responsible.

It is apparent that these different priorities represent the best way to ensure limited resources are shared between all those in need, with the community care officer's primary client being the elderly individual and their manager's primary clients being all those in their area needing a social care service. It would be undesirable for the community care officer to also be the budget holder as when assessing their individual client, as they would also have to consider all the other people to whom the authority was providing social care services, which could result in a conflict of interest. By separating the responsibility for undertaking the assessment of the individual's needs and allocating the budget, a conflict of interest is avoided.

Existential and humanistic ethics: action rooted in deliberation

Existentialism is a body of ideas that comes from ontology, or the study of being, which invites us to consider and confront the big questions about the nature and purpose of existence (Warnock, 1970). This can make some of us feel uncomfortable, insecure and avoidant. An early pioneer of existential thinking is the Danish philosopher Søren Kierkegaard (1813–55), but a more recent exponent of existential thinking is the French philosopher Jean-Paul Sartre (1905–80), whose works include *Being and Nothingness*

(1943), *Existentialism is a Humanism* (1946) and *Nausea* (1972). Existentialism offers a distinct view, a philosophy for life that is grounded in the knowable world, concerned with the experience of being – the lived experience. What is meant by the term 'knowable' in this context refers to a reality that is difficult to dispute without resorting to faith and speculative beliefs. For example, in Shakespeare's play *Hamlet*, there is a scene of a feast: there are tables, chairs, food and drink, and people having a merry time. None of this reality is disputed. Then, suddenly, the ghost of Hamlet's father appears to Hamlet – or so he claims, as only Hamlet can see him. So now an element of disputed reality is introduced. What are we to make of this? The options are:

a) ghosts exist and can appear only to specific individuals despite being amidst company.

b) Hamlet is mistaken, delusional, mentally ill or under the influence of hallucinogens.

For existentialists, only option (b) is viable as ghosts do not exist. Nor do God or gods; there is nothing in astrology, or any other metaphysical or paranormal phenomena, there is no guardian angel, holy father or mother that is somehow looking after us or our interests. Human existence is a no-frills, one-way flight that ends when we die. It is a journey into a universe that is completely indifferent to our existence. If this is the first time you have come across the ideas of existentialism, it can seem quite a bleak view of what it is to be alive; but, once understood it can be liberating. However, it does confer a lot of personal responsibility on each of us. Other important ideas of existentialism include the need to strive to be authentic or true to ourselves. We are totally responsible for ourselves and the decisions we make: we are free to make choices and choose a course of action – indeed, one could say we are condemned to do so, as there is no God, fate or destiny to which we can transfer this responsibility. 'Bad faith' is the term existentialists use to describe attempts to transfer or limit this responsibility by saying, 'I was provoked' or 'X made me do it' or 'It's the will of God' or 'It's my fate or destiny' or 'It was meant to be'. So we have free will or are condemned to have it, as we are solely responsible for ourselves, and we remake our ethics with every action.

Applications of existential thinking within health and social care

It can be a useful approach to challenge existing thinking and behaviour, as it is good for holding out the possibility of change and self-fulfilment so we are not condemned to repeat existing or historic patterns of thinking or behaviours. If we do repeat the same pattern of behaviour, whether it is domestic violence, substance misuse or offending, that is because we have *chosen* to repeat it. This is not an attempt to minimise the difficulty involved in changing established behaviour, but change is possible once responsibility for it is understood and accepted. However, challenge using existential thinking has limited potency and could even be offensive to people who have a strong belief in faith, fate or destiny.

Humanism

Closely associated with existentialism is humanism, a body of ideas maintaining that all experience is contained in human experience, and all expression of art and culture is the product of human creation. Like existentialism, it is an approach to life that is based on reason and is atheistic and secular. Humanism celebrates our common humanity and asserts that moral values are founded on human nature and experience alone. We could think of humanism like this: Carl Sagan the American astronomer, wrote a book called *The Pale Blue Dot*, which was what he named a photograph of the Earth, taken by the spacecraft *Voyager One* as it left our solar system. The Earth does indeed appear as a pale blue dot and contains all we know and have known, all the people who have ever lived or are significant to us. We are Earth bound; it is our home and the only place inhabited by humans. Humanists may hold events to mark a birth or a wedding or the life of someone who has died, known as humanist funerals. Such events are characterised by their celebration of the new life or relationship, or a life lived, and they avoid all reference to religion.

Applications of humanistic thinking in health and social care

Many people within the helping and caring professions are motivated by ideas derived from humanism. Early pioneers of these ideas include Abraham Maslow (1908–70) and Carl Rogers (1902–87), who were psychologists. Rogers was noted for having developed a form of humanistic psychotherapy known as person-centred counselling, in which – unlike psychoanalysis – the client and counsellor take a journey to explore their respective experiences and achieve their respective aspirations. The counsellor and their client enter a

> professional relationship based on equality, in which the counsellor has unconditional positive regard for their client. Examples of humanistic organisations include the Red Cross, the Hospice Movement and Medicine Sans Frontières (Medicine Without Borders), to name but a few.

Modernism: advancing and upholding universal principles, values and standards

The four schools of ethical philosophy discussed so far are products of a movement known as modernism, which itself derived from a distinct period of moral, philosophical and scientific development that took place in the United Kingdom and parts of Europe from the late 1700s up to the Industrial Revolution in an era known as the Enlightenment. People such as Voltaire, Hume, Locke and Newton are associated with this period. It is a largely Western, Eurocentric movement, and common themes that emerged were as follows.

- » *Reason.* The primacy of rationality and reason – the organising principle of knowledge tempered by experiment and experience. Linked to empiricism – the use of scientific method and reliable data.
- » *Empiricism.* Thought and knowledge based on empirical facts, known and comprehended through the recognised sense organs.
- » *Science.* Scientific knowledge based on repeatable experimental method. This is the basis upon which understanding and knowledge are determined.
- » *Universalism.* Reason and science applied equally to any and every situation, the derived laws of which govern the entire universe.
- » *Progress.* The quality of people's lives and the social conditions under which they live can be improved by the application of science and reason, leading to increasing happiness, well-being and rationally organised emancipation.
- » *Individualism.* Individual reason, authenticity and autonomy are the basis of thought and action.
- » *Toleration.* Promoting the concept of liberalism, toleration of religious and some moral convictions despite some inherent conflict with other ideas expressed in this list.
- » *Greater freedom.* In opposition to constraints on beliefs, trade, communication and social interaction and self-expression, previously imposed in feudal and more traditional times.

» *Uniformity.* The acceptance of the fact that human beings are basically the same, with the same needs.

» *Secularism.* Dividing the organs of the state – for example, separating government and religion, opposing traditional religious authority as the sole source of accepted knowledge and wisdom.

These ideas saw an end to the dark ages in which fear, ignorance and superstition played a significant role and paved the way for a 'new', 'modern' and contemporary world-view to emerge.

Another way to understand this time of transition is to consider a painting by the Derby artist Joseph Wright, (1734–97), whose painting *An Experiment with an Air Pump (1768)*, captures the eve of the beginning of this transition. The painting depicts a family scene, shrouded in gloom; there is no electric or gas light, so the room is lit by candlelight. At the centre is a table around which the family members are gathered to witness an intriguing spectacle. On the table stands a vacuum pump, connected to an inverted bell jar in which a dove is entrapped. The father is about to pump the air out of the bell jar, causing the bird to falter and collapse, as though dead, but he then quickly pumps air back into the jar and the dove appears to revive and come to life again. The observers knew something was happening before their eyes; they knew the father did not have powers to raise the dead but did not understand why what they were seeing happened. In 1768, the explanation was beyond their grasp of the knowledge required to comprehend what was going on. Oxygen was not discovered until 1774 and its association with haemoglobin and circulation was not understood until later, but this picture captures the cusp of discovery.

Radical ethics: challenging the status quo to promote justice and equality

The ideas behind radical ethics are characterised by the need to challenge normative power relations and the status quo, supporters of which consider to be organised to serve the interests of the ruling class and dominant gender. As such, they perpetrate injustice, structural discrimination and oppression, through poverty, social class, poor social mobility, a lack of life chances and equality of opportunity for a significant number of people. Perhaps the best-known example of radical ethics was derived from the work of Karl Marx (1818–83). His publications include *The Communist Manifesto* (1848) and *Capital* (1867, 1885 and 1894), in which he argues that the relationship between the capital owning class, which he termed the bourgeoisie, and the working class, which he termed the proletariat, was one of exploitation and conflict, illustrated by the capital-owning class having the power to close their business, making their workforce redundant and destroying their livelihoods. whereas all the workers could do was withdraw their labour through strike action. But radical ethics are not limited to critiques of the means of production; they apply wherever there is an organised challenge to the norm. Other examples include the feminist movement, which campaigns for equality between men and women; the Black Lives Matter movement, which opposes institutional racism; the 'Just stop oil' campaign, promoting action to address global warming; and 'eco warriors' and anti-vivisectionists, movements that seek to preserve the environment and promote animal welfare and rights, respectively.

Applications of radical ethics within health and social care

These are limited, but the view that people's problems originate from structural sources rather than dysfunction in an individual's pathology could be considered as being born from a radical perspective. A radical analysis would hold that improvement in social mobility and opportunity can only be brought about through political intervention to bring changes at a societal level, rather than relying on individual action to overcome poor life chances. Other forms of intervention and help would be pitched at group and community levels rather than individual casework – with an example being public health initiatives.

Observance to a higher authority through faith and religious belief

An example of a theologian's ethical philosophy can be found in the work of Thomas Aquinas (1224–1274). He was a Dominican priest who proposed that there were four kinds of law. One was eternal and the decree of God, which governs all creation. Another was natural law, which he thought of as human participation in the eternal law. This natural law tradition is the one reflected by the Catholic Church in its doctrines, and is the basis for the sanctity of marriage and procreation, hence the unacceptability of divorce and contraception for devout Catholics. Although not all religious belief comprises a school of ethical philosophy, like deontology or utilitarianism, the influence of how a particular God, or gods, the religious teachings of a particular religion on morality, or a religion's culture and practice will often dictate what is considered right or wrong; this is often of paramount importance to the devotees of that particular religion. As members of a multicultural society, we cannot hope to uphold our obligations, both moral and legal, to our fellow humans for whom their religious faith is an important part of their identity without a basic knowledge of this faith and be sensitive to its practices. I do not propose to set out this knowledge here; rather, I stress the importance for practitioners within health and social care to acquire it to a level appropriate to the scope of their intervention. For example, if your practice involves physical examination, you need to be aware of cultural and religious-based preferences of patients for practitioners of the same sex; there is also a reluctance to remove clothing, and the presence of a chaperone may be preferred. The considerations in this example may be particularly appropriate for female patients of Hindu or Islamic faith, although they are not necessarily restricted to these.

Other examples that require consideration for practice include the following.

» *Palliative care where religious practices differ regarding dying and death.* For example, Roman Catholics may want a priest to attend the dying to give the *last rites.* There are different practices for laying out the body – for example, a Muslim's head should be turned towards Mecca. There are issues about touch, washing and the removal of items on the body, and who should undertake this – for example, practitioners of the same sex as the dead person. The family members may wish to attend and also have their own spiritual leader attend – for example, for a Jew there would be a Rabbi in attendance.

» *Prayer.* For example, a devout Muslim may want to pray five times a day at particular times and may wish to wash before doing so. Their Holy day is Friday. Jews usually pray three times a day and their holy day is the Sabbath, which starts on Friday evening and ends on Saturday evening. During this time, devout Jews may not perform a range of certain tasks that are considered work.

» *Washing and personal hygiene.* Sikhs, Hindus and Muslims prefer washing in running water, so a shower is more appropriate than a bath. If they require assistance with this, they may prefer help from someone of the same sex.

» *Diet.* Dietary preferences extend beyond religious consideration as someone may be vegetarian, vegan or gluten intolerant, but there are also differences in what is acceptable in religious practices. For example, Jews and Muslims have particular rituals for the way meat is prepared (Kosher for Jews and Halal for Muslims). During the Muslim festival of Ramadan, Muslims should fast between sunrise and sunset. Some foodstuffs are restricted or forbidden – for example, pig and carrion for Muslims; pig, rabbit and shellfish for Jews. There are similar restrictions for Rastafarians. There are also issues about where food is prepared to avoid contamination. For example, Halal food should not be prepared in the same place as non-Halal food.

Acknowledging different beliefs

Some of the fundamental ideas enshrined in religious belief can present a challenge to those of different faiths or non-believers. Faiths that proclaim their God to be all-powerful, the sole orchestrator of creation, events and life, such as Christianity and Islam, have an awkward problem in the claim of an omnipotent God or Allah – if this is true, why do bad things happen? The only thing to conclude is because God wills them to happen, which produces cognitive dissonance with the notion of a beneficent God. Furthermore, if issues of life and death are solely the preserve of God, there are obvious implications for the acceptance of abortion, euthanasia, use of contraception and a variety of practices using the manipulation of genes and fertility, such as in vitro fertilisation (IVF).

Hinduism holds that although there is one god, this can take many forms. Central to Hinduism is the belief in reincarnation, but one's status and caste in the 'new' life is determined by one's behaviour in the previous life. This can produce some challenging consequences when viewed from a conventional Western perspective, such as the social ostracisation of the Dalit caste known as the untouchables. It is said that those of higher castes avoid the shadow of a Dalit falling on them. The only way for those in the Dalit caste to rid themselves of the discrimination to which they are subject appears to be to suffer it with humility throughout their current life in the hope of being born as a member of a higher caste in the next. Another potential outcome of this belief system concerns the birth of a disabled child, which is believed to be a consequence of errors or mistakes lived in a previous life (by the mother). It might seem somewhat unfair that the subsequent guilt and responsibility the parent may feel is unconnected to their current life, unlike the case of babies born with foetal alcohol syndrome or opiate dependency, where the mother has misused alcohol or drugs during her pregnancy and cause and effect has a more obvious connection.

For some religions, blood holds a special significance. Animals providing Halal and Kosher meat products must be slaughtered in a manner that drains the blood. There are particular practices surrounding women during menstruation in some religions. Perhaps the most striking practice regarding blood is the refusal of Jehovah's Witnesses to accept blood or its products, including transfusions, into the body – even in life-threatening situations. The fact that they would, for example, risk the life of a child by refusing them a transfusion seems alarming, but for those parents, allowing a blood transfusion would condemn the soul of the child to eternal damnation, whereas should the child without it, they will eventually be reunited for eternity in heaven.

Some of the cultural practices purportedly of some religions and their religious teachings appear to conflict with principles of liberal democracy, such as equality of opportunity and freedom of expression. The way some of these practices appear to discriminate against women compared with men in such matters as dress, showing hair, accessing education and work, as in the case of the Taliban in Afghanistan or the wearing of trousers or bras in respect of Boko Haram in Nigeria, can appear little more than male oppression of women. We may find it difficult to have respect for such practices, but we need to acknowledge them as, for example, we cannot assume all Muslim women regard the requirement for modesty in dress and presence as oppressive. On the contrary, it may be considered an expression of religious observance and compliance with cultural norms.

If we are unfamiliar with such practices, we may find them alien to our way of life. Yet we cannot deny their importance to those who think them right, proper and moral. Professionals delivering health and social care services need to be sensitive to, and educate themselves about, such beliefs so as not to cause offence or distress through making assumptions or ignorance. Further information on religions and considerations for health and social care practice can be found at www.interfaith.org.uk and www.bbc.co.uk/religion.

Postmodernism: recognition of diversity

The final set of ideas I want to introduce in this section on schools of ethical philosophy and traditions is postmodernism, which is really a movement that embodies a critical reflection on modernism, as discussed earlier in this chapter. Postmodernism challenges the claims of modernism by questioning and rejecting the ways in which the grand narratives such as universal human rights can be devised, implemented and upheld, provided that future generations wish to adopt them. Postmodernists would argue that the scope of difference and diversity between individuals, communities, cultures and nations is such that nothing can be considered *common* to the human condition, so nothing can be established that can be considered universal to it. In addition, it is critical of the degree of progress that has been achieved against that envisaged by the pioneers of the Enlightenment. Postmodernism is characterised by its focus on fragmentation (nothing is whole or connected; it is isolated and instable), relativism (the belief that 'truth' is relative to whoever is viewing it as such, so there is no absolute truth) and constructionism (meaning is derived from the mental and linguistic representations people give it, so a common understanding of a phenomenon is not possible). It is strong on the recognition of difference and diversity; however, it is considered nihilistic, negative and lacking in aspiration for humankind because there are no universal values or aims for which humans can collectively strive.

Notable postmodernist thinkers include Jean Francois Lyotard (1924–98), Michel Foucault (1926–84) and Jean Baudrillard (1929–2007).

Conclusion

I am aware that this chapter has been a challenging read, but I would encourage you to stick with it and come to grips with the ideas presented in it. Interventions in health and social care are as much about morality as they are about clinical skills. The ability to gain insights into where people are coming from promotes understanding and an appreciation of their perspectives. We will endure many frustrations in our professional lives, but understanding that many more of the decisions taken by a hospital's management will be influenced to a greater extent by utilitarian ethics than by your clinical practice working directly with patients and clients, which will be influenced to a greater extent by Kantian ethics, will reduce the potential for conflict – especially when we realise why both perspectives need to be represented and given their respective emphasis.

While we should acquaint ourselves with some of the basic customs, culture and beliefs likely to be held and practised by the members of the community we serve so that we can provide culturally sensitive practice, we cannot know everything – so if you are in doubt, is it far better to ask than to assume.

Chapter 4 | Medical ethics

Consideration of what should constitute medical ethics dates as far back as the Greek and Roman era. An early example is the oath attributed to the ancient Greek physician Hippocrates. In taking the Hippocratic Oath, the physician pledges to prescribe only beneficial treatments according to their abilities and judgement; to refrain from causing harm or hurt; and to live an exemplary personal and professional life. The oath is still taken by doctors at graduation ceremonies in many medical schools today.

In any consideration of medical ethics, it would be remiss not to acknowledge the work of Beauchamp and Childress. The eighth edition of their book *Principles of Biomedical Ethics* was published in 2019 (their first being in 1977) and they are pioneers of the modern application of ethics in medicine. Beauchamp and Childress have gone on to make a significant contribution in the field. Medical ethics does, however, have a long tradition. The first comprehensive account of the topic in the United Kingdom was written by the physician Thomas Percival (1803), titled *Medical Ethics*. Beauchamp and Childress cite four clusters of moral principles, which they assert '*are central to biomedical ethics*' (Beauchamp and Childress, 2019, p 13). They are respect for autonomy, non-maleficence, beneficence and justice.

Respect for autonomy

Most of us would recognise the visceral drive we have to establish and maintain our autonomy and have it respected. Respect for autonomy comes in a variety of guises – for example, the principle of client self-determination or regard for our wishes and feelings. But can this be absolute? While it conforms with the principle of respect for autonomy to seek to maximise a person's expression of autonomy or self-rule by complying with their wishes and feelings, there are circumstances in which this cannot be total; in others, it is restricted or severely compromised. As Beauchamp and Childress (2019, p 99) assert, '*the principle of respect for the autonomous choices of persons runs as deep in morality as any principle, but determining its nature, scope and strength requires careful analysis*'. They propose two conditions for autonomy: liberty (independence from controlling influences) and agency (capacity for intentional action) (Beauchamp and Childress, 2019, p 100).

A parent's authority over their child is absolute at birth but diminishes with age. Once a child is considered Gillick competent – being able to weight decision-making rationally, with an understanding of the issues involved and the consequences – their views should be sought and, in liberal interpretations, complied with. They are establishing their sense of autonomy through adolescence, which is fully acknowledged when they reach the age of majority (18 years). However, there are circumstances where a parent's authority over their baby is not absolute but disputed. Charlie Gard was born with a rare and fatal genetic disease. Before he reached the age of one, the hospital treating him applied to the family court for a judgment on whether it would be lawful to withdraw artificial ventilation and provide palliative care. His parents wanted treatment to continue. Charlie's views, although unobtainable, were represented by a guardian appointed by the court. When Article 8: Right to Family Life (*Human Rights Act 1998*) and *s 1 (1)* of the *Children Act 1989*, which states that 'the child's welfare shall be the court's paramount consideration' in its decision-making, were applied, the court found subjecting him to further treatment would cause distress and significant harm and ruled in favour of the hospital. Treatment was withdrawn and Charlie died.

There are circumstances where one's autonomy is diminished or restricted or not ascertainable or exercised against medical opinion. This may be through congenital learning disability or mental impairment due to accident or illness, such as stroke or dementia, or mental health diagnosis. In cases of coma or persistent vegetative state, the wishes and feelings of the patient are not ascertainable and in the absence of any advance directive, the best option is to consult the family or loved ones of the patient regarding what may have been the patient's wishes and feelings about their care. In the case of someone with dementia, a ward or care home may have an external door locked to prevent them from wandering, which is clearly a restriction of their liberty but justified to prevent harm. However, their view may be sought regarding they would like to wear, or eat for breakfast that day, maximising the extent to which they are able to exercise autonomy. Under the *Mental Capacity Act 2005*, if someone is assessed as having capacity, they are also able to make unwise decisions – for example, an asthma sufferer being determined to keep their dog despite its fur exacerbating their condition, or a person with emphysema continuing to smoke. It would be quite wrong for their respiratory advisers to insist that the dog be re-homed, or they must stop smoking, but these may be actively suggested. However, what about a person living alone whose house is a fire risk through hoarding or is falling into severe disrepair, and evidence exists that they are neglecting their own health and wellbeing? Some of these issues may be addressed through the provision of home care so the person is able to maintain their independence, but if this is refused, the suggestion of respite or residential care might need to be made. This situation becomes a dilemma as intervention cannot be compulsory where the person concerned has capacity; equally, it is very difficult for health and social care services to stand by and simply witness their neglect.

The way forward lies in discussion about what would be acceptable to improve the situation. In another example, the liberty and autonomy of those on remand or serving a prison sentence is deemed to be legitimately restricted as the forfeit for being accused or having committed crimes against society.

Beauchamp and Childress (2019, p 102) identify three conditions that need to be present for autonomy to be exercised, and help to analyse the nature, scope and strength of it. They are intentionality, understanding and the absence of controlling influences. Someone could be said to be exercising their autonomy where they intend to act or do something in a planned, deliberate manner, possess a rational understanding of the act and why they want to execute it, and appreciate any consequences arising from it. While no one is forcing them to execute the act, they may feel they have responsibilities or obligations to people but their action is freely carried out.

Non-maleficence

At its simplest this principle states 'above all (or first) do no harm'. However, we need not delve far into practice before we run into problems. Cases of medical negligence occur when the conduct of the practitioner falls below a standard of due care. Beauchamp and Childress (2019, p 160) cite four essential elements that need to be present for cases to be proven:

1. *The professional must have a duty to the affected party.*
2. *The professional must breach that duty.*
3. *The affected party must experience a harm.*
4. *The harm must be caused by that breach of duty.*

Professional malpractice occurs when a therapeutic relationship proves harmful or unhelpful, provided that the practitioner concerned has failed to follow their professional standards of care. In cases of proven negligence and professional malpractice, the principle of non-maleficence has clearly been breached. But what about treatment that involves risk of harm, or medication that has deleterious side-effects, or the withholding or withdrawing treatment. Withholding means not starting, whereas withdrawing means stopping, and seems the more deliberate of the two acts despite their having a similar result. Difficult decisions are made every day concerning seriously ill patients and around end-of-life care, consideration of the overall intent regarding the patient's welfare, prognosis and further suffering or distress being caused through, for example, life-sustaining treatment such as resuscitation or intravenous lines being used to provide nutrition and hydration, which serve to buffer the charge of breaching the non-maleficence principle. The administration of morphine in end-of-life care may ease suffering but also hasten death. In such deliberations, the overall benefits to the patient must be weighed as greater than any deleterious effects to conform to the obligation of non-maleficence. As we saw with the Charlie Gard case, what may be considered in the best interest of children can be contested. It is one thing for an adult member of the Jehovah's Witnesses faith refusing a lifesaving blood transfusion for themselves, but quite another if they refuse consent for their non-Gillick competent child to have the transfusion. In such circumstances, medics may look to the courts for a ruling. Whether the issue is about refusing treatment or insisting on continuing it when doing so would not be in the best interests of the child, such cases are controversial and have the potential to create conflict between the clinician's duty to the primary client (the child) and that owed towards secondary and tertiary clients (immediate and extended family). Advances in technology enabling a greater degree of survivability for serious chronic conditions are likely to make such decision-making even more complex. Although physician assisted dying is currently illegal in the United Kingdom, there is a call for parliament to consider euthanasia again. Should it be made legal at some point in the future, the physician's obligation to uphold the non-maleficence principle will need revising to allow respect for autonomy to override it.

Beneficence

So far, we have an obligation to respect autonomy and avoid doing harm, but what about a positive obligation to do good? This is where the principle of beneficence comes in. Within this principle's scope fall several prima facie rules of obligation under beneficence. Beauchamp and Childress (2019, p 219) cite the following:

1. *Protect and defend the rights of others.*
2. *Prevent harm from occurring to others.*
3. *Remove conditions that will cause harm to others.*
4. *Help persons with disabilities.*
5. *Rescue persons in danger.*

Beneficence is implicit in the overall aim of the provision of health and social care services. It underpins the motives, initiatives and actions taken by practitioners in helping their clients, patients and the general public through public health. It differs from non-maleficence in a couple of ways: it calls for positive action rather than simply the avoidance of something, and it is open-ended, in that precisely what you may do to help someone is not usually stated unless specified for a particular condition or treatment. Accordingly, in general terms there are no punitive measures imposed for not doing enough to help someone, as in the case of proven professional malpractice and medical negligence. It is not easy to specify which actions of beneficence may be considered optional against those that may be considered obligatory. However, although the limits to what you can do to help may not be specified, they are implicit in the practical application of utilitarian ethics that any public body such as the NHS must employ. What is offered by way of treatment will be governed by the level of knowledge and technical innovation available, and its affordability at any given time. For example, the National Institute for Health and Care Excellence (NICE) is a body that provides guidance on the most efficacious treatment of a host of conditions and diseases. It also makes evidence-based recommendations for the health and social care sector, developed by independent committees comprising both professional and lay members. For example, it recommended in March 2023 that a weight-loss drug named Semaglutide be made available for some patients in specialist NHS services. This treatment costs approximately £954 annually per patient, and its use is restricted, only being prescribed to those with a body mass index in excess of at least 30 kg/m^2. In 2019, the health survey for England estimated that 28 per cent of adults in England were obese and currently costing £6.1 billion to the NHS annually (Holmes, 2021). NICE had to balance the cost of the new treatment against the cost to the NHS that would otherwise be incurred by it not being made available. Helen Knight, director of medicine evaluation at NICE, said, *'Semaglutide won't be available to everyone. Our committee has made specific recommendations to ensure it remains value for money for the taxpayer and will only be prescribed for a maximum of two years'* (NICE, 2023).

A note about paternalism

Straddling the territory between respect for autonomy and beneficence lies the potential for paternalism, which means to act like a father in thinking that the practitioner knows best or assumes they do, and that they will act in the best interests of their client or patient without the need to fully consult them to obtain their wishes and feelings, and thus deny or limit respect for their client's autonomy. The same applies to care tasks where the carer does not allow those cared for to undertake tasks of which they are capable and may prefer to undertake themselves. Of course, there are situations where paternalism is not only appropriate but necessary. These are where non-Gillick competent children are involved or the patient or client does not have capacity, or their capacity is limited through congenital learning disability, physical disability, brain injury, illness or disease. In cases where capacity is limited, every effort should be made to ascertain the client's or patient's wishes and feelings where they can express a meaningful choice. We discussed earlier the case of a person with dementia whose liberty was restricted due to risk of harm if allowed to wander. It would not be appropriate to seek the patient's view about the need to restrict liberty, as allowing them the freedom to wander is not an option, but they may be able to exercise choice in what they want to wear or eat for breakfast. Where people have capacity, it is incumbent on the practitioner to take the time and go to the trouble to give the patient or client the information they need to be able to make informed choices and decisions, in which any pros and cons are weighed to minimise paternalism and maximise respect for autonomy.

Justice

The fourth and final principle of medical ethics is justice. Justice can seem an abstract concept until we recognise it through others being subject to injustice or ourselves; then it becomes very real. Civil courts can grant a range of orders that seek to protect children based on their having suffered or being likely to suffer 'significant harm'. When the wording in this piece of legislation was proposed in parliament, discussion took place about its definition. It was suggested that people would know it when they saw it. As a notion, justice is similar. If we are unlawfully discriminated against or feel we have been treated unfairly or without the degree of consideration to which we feel we are entitled, we have a keen sense of injustice. It is incumbent on health and social care practitioners to uphold the rights of their clients and patients and ensure they are not treated unjustly. Moreover, the benefits – for example, in a standard treatment or intervention (at any one point in time) – need to be distributed fairly and equitably among those who are eligible, without preferential treatment or treatment that has a deleterious effect on any particular group. We can see the need to include justice within medical ethics through the examples given in the following paragraph, where patients were not afforded justice in the treatment they received. There are some specific challenges to this general rule. For example, in clinical trials for new drugs in which there may be a control group that either receives the drug or a placebo, the volunteers themselves may not know which option they are taking; in double-blind trials, the researchers running the test may not know either, but provided the volunteers are fully informed of the aims and risks of the trial, and have capacity to give their informed consent, there is no breach of the principle. Although practitioners need to ensure they treat their patients and clients in a just manner, the concept does not solely relate to them. We saw how NICE had to carefully weigh up the benefits of new medicines being available against the cost to the public purse, as taxpayers also need to be recipients of justice.

Why do we need ethics in medicine?

The whole enterprise of providing health and social care services to our fellow citizens is a moral endeavour. Therefore, ethical considerations are central to practice. Another answer is the same as the reason given to the question about why we need ethics, appropriate values and rights in health and social care generally, which is to impose acceptable professional standards to reduce the chance of anything less passing for practice. Despite the Hippocratic Oath, and the establishment of moral principles through medical ethics, there have been examples of unethical medical interventions involving quality of care, treatment and research methodology. These include the following (Hawley, 2007, p 6).

- » *Willowcreek School, USA (1963–66).* This was a residential school for children with physical or learning disabilities who were deliberately infected (by injection) with hepatitis A to see how quickly the disease spread and to test the efficacy of treatments.

- » *Tuskegee, USA (1932–72).* This concerned a 40-year-long experiment to study the difference in people with syphilis between those being treated with penicillin and those who were not. A public health nurse helped to persuade 400 African American men with syphilis to forgo taking penicillin, despite it having already been tested, available and being the standard treatment for the disease. The patients were not aware of their rights, nor had their informed consent been sought (see Chapter 6).

- » *National Woman's Hospital, New Zealand (1958–87).* This involved 948 women who had cervical cancer being divided into two groups: one group received treatment for the disease while the other did not. This resulted in some unnecessary disfigurement and death of patients (see Cartwright Inquiry, 1988).

- » *Chelmsford Hospital, Sydney, Australia.* This involved people with psychiatric illnesses being prescribed medication that would result in deep sedation for days on end. This 'deep sleep' treatment was ostensibly to 'cure' their illnesses; far from doing that, however, it resulted in a range of serious medical conditions, some of which resulted in death (see Royal Commission into Deep Sleep Therapy, 1990).

- » *Bristol Royal Infirmary Inquiry (1984–95), also known as the Bristol Heart Inquiry.* A number of babies and children who required cardiac surgery were found not to have been given a correct standard of care and many died as a result. Problems found included a lack of insight, flawed behaviour and ineffective communication among clinical practitioners (see Bristol Royal Infirmary Inquiry, 2001).

These examples may be considered outstanding in their failure of patient care. Nevertheless, they demonstrate how ethical practice can slide into callous disregard for the welfare of patients, their autonomy and rights. Ethical practice cannot be taken for granted but is remade in every ward of every hospital and health-care setting every day by the decisions and actions of its practitioners.

Infected Blood Inquiry Final Report 2024

Serving to underscore the importance of the previous paragraph, on 20 May 2024, the final Report of the Independent Infected Blood Inquiry was published, having been requested by the government in 2017. It exposed a shocking scandal in which, in the United Kingdom between 1970 and 1998, patients were given transfusions and blood products that were infected with HIV and Hepatitis C, B and D. About 30,000 of them contracted these infections and, of these, about 3000 have already died from these diseases. The author of the report and chairperson of the inquiry said in a summary statement, 'I have also to report a systemic, collective and individual failures to deal ethically, appropriately and quickly with the risk of infections being transmitted in blood, with the infections when materialised and with the consequences for thousands of families.'

The blood had been purchased from a variety of sources to meet a demand that was not met from sources within the United Kingdom. These included American prisoners, many of whom were intravenous drug users who had contracted HIV and hepatitis. The report identifies a failure to acknowledge that these patients should not have been infected, an absence of any meaningful apology or redress, the use of inaccurate, misleading and defensive lines, and a lack of openness, transparency and candour by the NHS and successive governments, which conspired to hide the truth over several decades and refused any accountability or the provision of compensation. Patients were treated without discussion about risk or available alternatives, so their informed consent to treatment could not have been obtained.

This episode marks the worse and most significant example of medical negligence in the history of the NHS. It consisted of operational, administrative and clinical errors as well as in research, but also an absence of appropriate values, ethics and the upholding of patients' rights, which are essential for a safe and effective health service.

The government is now committed to launching a compensation scheme for the surviving victims and the families of those who have died as a result of receiving infected blood (UK Government, 2024).

Case study

What should have happened

If NHS England could wind the clock back and begin their response at the point of it needing additional blood and blood products again, an ethical approach would have looked something like the following. The NHS is, of course, obliged to procure what it needs to treat its patients, but it has choices about how it does this. In the case of blood and blood products, it may be preferable to source supplies from the indigenous population, by voluntary donation. This is what usually happens but in the event of this providing insufficient supplies, there could have been a national campaign to boost donations, rather than obtaining supplies outside of the UK and buying it from people who may be keen to sell it. Whichever method of sourcing supplies is chosen there must be efficacious methods for its screening, for blood group type, quality and contamination (including infection), transportation and storage. With any such an important procurement an assessment of risk should be undertaken to ensure this remains manageable. In the event of some degree of risk being present, despite effective screening, this risk, along with likely consequences and alternatives, should be discussed with patients in order to obtain their informed consent. Finally, if a mistake has occurred resulting in harm, action to address it should occur immediately with adequate redress, including appropriate compensation made promptly.

Ethical dilemmas

The current position taken by the UK Government regarding euthanasia (where a physician administers a lethal drug to a patient who has requested it) and physician-assisted dying (where the physician prepares the lethal drug, but the patient administers it) is that both are illegal. If a physician or anyone else performs either action, they are committing a criminal offence. Withholding or withdrawing treatment, even if this causes or hastens death, is considered passive euthanasia and is not necessarily illegal, provided it can be justified by medical opinion as being in the overall best interests of the patient, to relieve suffering where the prospects for recovery are poor. Administering treatment intended to relieve pain but with the foreseen result that it is likely to shorten life is normally legal, provided it is done in the patient's best interest; if a patient who has capacity refuses life-saving treatment, this is not considered to be suicide and the physician is not assisting suicide by acceding to the patient's wishes – in fact, they would be committing battery, a form of assault, if they ignored them and administered the treatment. Countries in which euthanasia and assisted dying are lawful include Belgium, The Netherlands, Switzerland, New Zealand, Australia and Canada.

An ethical dilemma occurs when an ethical problem does not have an entirely satisfactory solution, irrespective of the perspective from which it is viewed. Ethical dilemmas often produce debates on topics, the 'sides' of which tend to be polarised between those who are for a proposal or idea and those who are against it. Euthanasia is a topic that has produced such a debate. Arguments for include the following.

» *The promotion of personal autonomy.* Under the *Human Rights Act 1998*, citizens have a right to life (Article 2). Although this right is limited – in that there are exceptions such as in the execution of a sentence, imposed by a court following conviction of a crime, or shot in defence from violence (by a police officer) – it is a positive duty to protect life. However, there is no corresponding right to be in control of one's own death, at a place and time of one's choosing.

» *In the interest of justice.* In the United Kingdom, we do not have a right to die. It is denied us because it is illegal. This means we may have to suffer the intolerable pain and distress that serious debilitating illness can bring. We are prevented having the right to bring this to a dignified end if we choose to and accept something with which we may disagree. Our only option would be to travel to a country where euthanasia is lawful, such as Switzerland or Belgium, and if we did so it would need to be at a time when we were well enough to travel and be denied dying in the comfort of our own home or local hospice.

» *Choice.* Existentialists and humanists want the option of choosing euthanasia, or assisted dying, as it is congruent with their personal values of taking ownership of their life and responsibility for it.

The arguments against include the following.

» Religious beliefs in the sanctity of life and that only God in the Christian faith, or Allah in Islam, has the authority to give or take life.

» Improvements in palliative care and pain management in all but the most severe cases, which make euthanasia an unnecessarily drastic step.

» The potential for abuse, which cannot be reduced to zero. Some vulnerable people could feel coerced into euthanasia, either directly or indirectly – for example, by relatives wishing to speed up their receipt of inheritance, or free themselves of caring responsibilities, or the person concerned feeling they are a burden, which could influence their decision.

But these issues are rarely clear cut and increase in complexity and ambiguity the further we delve into them. For example, the human-granted 'right to life' (Article 2 of the *Human Rights Act 1998*) and the religious-based sanctity of life are compromised by interpretation about when life actually starts. As it is lawful to have an abortion up to 24 weeks of pregnancy in the United Kingdom, are we to assume it starts at the

25th week of gestation? Furthermore, in IVF treatment, some of the fertilised eggs may be discarded, with only one or two being transferred into the womb. There are also problems about when life ends. Some people give advance directives or make living wills when they have the capacity to express their wishes about what they want to happen; however, how does this apply later in life when they might not have capacity – for example, if they have advanced dementia – in circumstances where their life, or quality of life is threatened by illness, disease or nearing death? It would be difficult to argue that anyone in a persistent vegetive state has any quality of life, but is it right to withdraw liquid or nutrition or switch off life-support systems? People also sometimes express a wish not to be resuscitated in certain circumstances, and clinical decisions are made about this. Hawley (2007, p 205) makes a distinction between active and passive euthanasia: the former is an action taken to deliberately end life, such as the administration of a muscle relaxant to stop the heart following an induced coma; the latter refers to the omission of acting to prolong life, such as the withholding of fluids or nutrition. It may be a moot point, as both routes produce the same outcome.

Case study

Ethical dilemmas

You are a nurse working on an acute medical ward and oncology clinic. One of your patients has cancer of the oesophagus, which was in remission but has now returned, and his consultant has recently told him his illness is terminal and he has a few months left to live. This patient shared his prognosis with you and initially appeared quite philosophical about his news, however some days later he asks for a private conversation with you and disclosed that he is deeply troubled and distressed at the prospect of slowly dying of this condition. Swallowing food is already causing some discomfort and the idea of feeding tubes being directly inserted into his stomach while he continues to deteriorate appals him. He says he wants to be in control of this process and he asks you to undertake some research as to how he might access the services of Dignitas in Switzerland. You suggest that such thoughts may best be discussed with family. He explained that he tried to discuss it with his wife who was totally opposed to the idea, saying she wanted him to live for as long as possible and as a Catholic she considered those who took their own lives to be condemning themselves to eternal damnation. He pleads with you to help him. On a personal level you can understand him and feel sympathetic to his request but as a nurse you are committed to do no harm and feel conflicted. You suggest he uses the internet but again he says would need your help to do this. You explain as a nurse your duty is to do no harm, but he denies helping him would cause harm, on the contrary it would bring him some consolation. You don't want to refuse him but are worried that complying with his request could be seen as aiding and abetting euthanasia.

A sensible solution to this dilemma would be to avoid giving an answer straight away and say you need to seek the view of your clinical supervisor, which would likely confirm that you could not compromise your duty to promote the health and wellbeing of your patients.

Exercise

» Express your thoughts on euthanasia.

» Are you for or against it and why?

» If you are for euthanasia, what checks and balances would you want to put in place to prevent abuse?

The other ethical dilemma explored in this chapter is eugenics. The eugenics movement started around 1883 and continues, in various forms, to the present day. At its simplest, the movement promotes the notion that the human race could and should strengthen its genome by the manipulation of genetics and the scientific laws of inheritance. It has used – some would say misused – the work of the pioneer of evolutionary theory Charles Darwin and geneticist Gregor Mendel to argue for the idea of racial improvement. Such a notion inevitably leads to discrimination against those individuals or groups whose contribution to the gene pool is considered to weaken it or be undesirable. The more extreme eugenicists, in seeking a perfect society, have identified those groups and individuals they consider unfit to reproduce, including ethnic and religious minorities, people with disabilities, the urban poor and LGBTQ+ individuals.

Francis Galton (1822–1911) is considered to be the father of eugenics. He coined the term, meaning 'good in stock' and set out its basic ideas in his book, *Inquiries into Human Fertility and its Development* (Galton, 1907). Charles Davenport (1866–1944) was another significant proponent of selective reproduction and its restriction for certain individuals and groups. The movement established itself most notably in America, and some states passed laws permitting enforced sterilisation. Perhaps the darkest manifestation of the idea behind eugenics was born through the work of the

German biologist Alfred Ploetz, whose book *Basic Principles of Racial Hygiene* (Ploetz, 1895) was influential in Nazi ideology regarding Nordic and Aryan racial superiority, and the incarceration and attempted genocide of certain groups, including the Jews.

So far, the ideas behind eugenics do not look like they present much of a debate, let alone an ethical dilemma, as most members of liberal democracies would find the consequences, if not the ideas themselves, unacceptable or even abhorrent. But let's consider this a little more holistically. Few would deny the benefit of a wheat crop that has increased resistance to pests and disease or has shorter stalks and higher yields. The genetic modification of plants and animals, although remaining controversial for some, has brought significant dividends in food production for human consumption. But what about humans?

In the United Kingdom, the Human Fertility and Embryology Authority governs research and practice, whereas the *Human Fertilisation and Embryology Acts 1990* and *2008* make legal provision for reproductive services. Clearly, there is manipulation of reproduction through IVF treatment and, while it may be possible to receive one or two attempts through the NHS, the cost of a private cycle is approximately £4000 to £7000, so one could argue that some selection is taking place based on the ability to pay. An amniocentesis test may be offered to pregnant women thought to have a higher chance of having a baby with a genetic condition. The test can diagnose several conditions, including Down's syndrome, cystic fibrosis and muscular dystrophy, to name but three. The choice is given to the mother to continue with the pregnancy or abort the foetus should the test be positive for one of the conditions. In 2013, a court in London approved the sterilisation of a 36 year-old man known as DE, whose IQ – in the region of 40, equivalent to the mental age of a six- to nine-year-old – was considered capable of consenting to sex but not able to make an informed decision about contraception. Justice Eleanor King considered his rights under Article 8 of the European Court of Human Rights and powers under Section 4 of the *Mental Health Act 2005* and ruled that it was in his best interest to have a vasectomy. DE was considered not to have the capacity to choose or refuse the procedure or to litigate on his own behalf. In 2016, a baby was born who had genetic material from three people. The baby inherited most of his DNA from his mother and father, but a third person also contributed. The mother carried a fatal illness in her mitochondria that the baby would have inherited. This part of her DNA was exchanged with that from a healthy donor, preventing the baby from developing the illness.

The four examples described above, it could be argued, represent morally ethical applications of eugenics. But what is the extent to which eugenics might to applied ethically? Enabling parenthood for couples of wanted children and disabling parenthood for those incapable of caring for children or wanting to avoid serious illness or disability may be justifiable, although some may find this contentious. But what about parents who present wanting their foetuses to be screened, selected or their genetics changed for certain physical characteristics, or personality traits or enhanced intelligence? Unlike animal husbandry, in which selective breeding has been taking place for centuries, human genetics is a relatively new science, but the mapping of the human genome and technical improvements in sequencing and its manipulation are likely to present new possibilities and dilemmas with which medical ethicists will doubtless have to grapple in the not-too-distant future. Whatever the outcome of such challenges, the debates and decisions about what is and is not acceptable will fall within the province of ethics.

Exercise

» Give your thoughts on eugenics.
» In what ways do you think it can offer benefits to humankind?
» What safeguards might you want in place so its application remains ethical?

Other perspectives on euthanasia and eugenics

Finally, before we conclude this chapter, let's briefly revisit some of the schools of ethical philosophy and traditions introduced in Chapter 3 to see how they might view euthanasia and eugenics if considered through their perspective.

Kantian ethics is about converting ideas into what could become acceptable universal laws. It is also very clear that humans should never be treated as a means to an end, but rather as an end in themselves, as anything else would taint the quality of their treatment. So, there is nothing in principle against euthanasia provided it is chosen by the recipient, with full capacity and knowledge about the procedure and its consequences – or, if the recipient lacked capacity, a decision was made that could be regarded as in their best interest, and not simply pragmatism. The position in respect of eugenics is similar to that concerning euthanasia. There must be strong safeguards in place to ensure that its application is not born of discrimination against an individual or group, or degenerates into it, as this would be using it as a means to an end and would not conform to the universal law test.

An action that is right for utilitarians is one that produces an outcome that is the best option for a majority. Let's say the government held a referendum on euthanasia. If it showed that a majority of people in the United Kingdom thought euthanasia was a good thing, the UK government ought to change the law and make it legal. However, if the vote was 52 per cent for and 48 per cent against, then a significant minority could be subject to the practice. Now let's say an analysis showed the 52 per cent who voted for it were found to be under 45 years of age, and those who voted against it were found to be over 60 years of age. Let's now imagine the economy of the United Kingdom was such that younger people were struggling to get high paid jobs and buy houses and pay taxes that were used to pay the pensions and fund the health care of over 60 year-olds. In a utilitarian world, a decision to introduce compulsory euthanasia for over 60 year-olds could be justified.

The outcome regarding eugenics would be similar. The example I gave Chapter 1 about ridding the world of Huntington's Chorea could be applied. If a majority thought it was a good outcome for those suffering with the disease or carrying the gene for its transmission (a minority) to be either forcibly sterilised, or otherwise prevented from perpetuating the disease, then it would be the morally right thing to do.

If you are a little uncomfortable about the potential consequences of utilitarianism, you've understood a significant weakness, in that there are no safeguards for the rights of the minority. So a dictator could come to power in a country and convince the majority of the population that a minority group within that population was bad, the other, or the enemy; the development of labour, concentration or extermination camps would not be far away. Sadly, human history is rife with such examples.

Existential and humanistic ethics is about taking responsibility and becoming the captain of our own ship, so in principle there is no objection to either euthanasia or eugenics. To some extent, you could say these movements were manifestly about taking control and exercising responsibility within a secular framework, so to some extent they are in harmony with existential and humanistic ethics provided effective rules and regulation are in place to respect individual wishes and uphold human rights.

Modernism and its opposite, postmodernism, are movements rather than schools of ethical philosophy, and as such do not take a firm stance on topics such as euthanasia and eugenics. However, we could say that modernism would be confident that ethical and effective policy, procedure, rules and regulation *could* be devised and could serve human beings on phenomena such as euthanasia and eugenics, whereas postmodernism would cast doubt on the assertion that we could.

Radical ethics would be manifest in taking up strongly held views on these topics and campaigning for or against euthanasia or eugenics to challenge and change existing law and practice.

Observance of a higher authority would mean that your view on euthanasia or eugenics would be dictated by whatever the religious teaching, creeds and texts of that particular higher authority said on the matter. If, for example, this was traditional or orthodox in that only God, Allah or Jehovah was deemed able to give or take life, impose infertility, illness and disease, or bless someone with children and good health, and the will of God, Allah or Jehovah had to be accepted, then any human meddling in the mechanics of such matters would be wrong and sinful. If, however, a more liberal interpretation of scripture were allowed or tolerated, it could be said that the higher power had given humanity the ingenuity to do x or y and, provided that human intervention was not regarded as usurping the authority of the higher power, a little more flexibility may be afforded.

Conclusion

This chapter has highlighted some disturbing examples of the treatment of patients in which the practice to which they were subject lost any consideration of medical ethics. The examples used achieved some degree of notoriety due to their being cited in textbooks. They may be considered exceptional, but they should not be regarded as unique or confined to history. Any intervention within health and social care has the potential to fail to meet the standard the profession concerned sets out to achieve. So how can practitioners safeguard their practice against such slippage? We need look no further than Kant. If we pledge that our duty to our patients and clients is to offer them the best service according to our skills and abilities, and if we make this our maxim for our professional lives, we will safeguard our practice from becoming less than we would want for ourselves, those we care about and the standards to which we aspire.

Chapter 5 | Rights: their role in countering discrimination and oppression

Rights

Chapters 2, 3 and 4 have demonstrated why it is of crucial importance to the quality of professional practice that workers in health and social care adopt and comply with appropriate values and ethics, in accordance with the standards and codes of conduct that govern their occupation. The same goes for rights, for how can practitioners uphold the rights of their clients and patients unless they are familiar with the rights to which their clients and patients are entitled? This chapter considers rights and entitlements, and the role they play in countering unfair treatment and unlawful discrimination. It is longer than the other chapters in this book, but I ask the reader to bear with it as there are sound reasons for what is presented. The chapter begins with a short section on the history and nature of the development of rights, which is included to show how we have arrived at the current provision of rights and entitlements available to us. The remainder of the chapter is connected, as Article 14 of the *Human Rights Act 1998* leads to the further development of equality legislation through the *Equality Act 2010*, which in turn requires further discussion about discrimination. We all need a basic understanding of these, both as citizens of the United Kingdom and as service provider to clients and patients.

What do we mean by a right?

The *Concise Oxford English Dictionary* defines a right as '*a thing one may legally or morally claim; the state of being entitled to a privilege or immunity or authority to act*'. For example, if you are a student at university and have a disability that complies with the provisions of the *Equality Act 2010*, you would have a legal right to gain access to the campus and its buildings; correspondingly, the university would have a duty to make *reasonable adjustments* to enable your participation. You have a moral right to have your work assessed and marked fairly. Despite having these rights, an element of subjectivity in interpretation cannot be eradicated completely. For example, there must be an assessment made of what constitutes reasonable in terms of the adjustments the university is obliged to make for a particular person's disability, and the teaching team may try to minimise significant differences between markers through standardisation and moderation processes, yet minor differences are likely to remain. Of course, the existence of this element does not necessarily mean the person with the disability has been unlawfully discriminated against or the work unfairly marked. But the need to make a judgement is ever-present in such matters, so the potential for discrimination or unfairness exists.

How might we recognise the need for a right?

The development of rights in both the United Kingdom and other parts of the world has evolved over time to include a comprehensive range of activities and situations in which we may find ourselves, from the quest for equality in things like equal pay for women for the same work, to safeguarding in areas as diverse as health and safety, child protection and deprivation of liberty for the vulnerable, race relations and employment. These rights have usually been enshrined in primary legislation and regulations by governments. There are also other bodies with a mandate to draft rules and conventions, including the United Nations; the signatories to these agree to honour them. In the United Kingdom, the recognition of the need for a right has often been due to the treatment of an individual or group being considered unfair or unjust. Much of the progress made in the development of protection against discrimination has been piecemeal, often being campaigned for by the individuals or group subject to the unfair or unjust treatment. For example, in 1999 four individuals were dismissed from their jobs in the armed forces simply because they were gay or lesbian. They took their case to the European Court of Human Rights, which ruled that they had been unfairly discriminated against. This ruling led to the United Kingdom – which was then a signatory to the UN Convention on Human Rights so had agreed to comply with its articles – changing its domestic law through the Employment Equality (Sexual Orientation) Regulations 2003 (since revoked, as protection is now afforded through the *Equality Act 2010*). The four servicemen and women were reinstated. While rights of individuals or groups can be conferred through legislation, legislation can also be used to oppress and discriminate against individuals or groups – for example, the pass laws in South Africa during the apartheid regime, which restricted the movement of the non-white population and laws in many US states that enforced racial segregation. An example of segregation in the United States occurred through an act of civil disobedience. In 1955, in Montgomery, Alabama, Rosa Parks, a seamstress in a local department store, was tired after her day's work and boarded a bus for her trip home. Seating on the bus was segregated, with whites towards the front and seating for people of colour toward the rear. As more white people boarded the bus, the driver asked Rosa to move further back down the bus, but she refused to give up her seat, contrary to state law. Her protest led to a boycott of the bus company and represented an early campaign of the civil rights movement in America. Momentum gathered over time and resulted in change through the 1964 Civil Rights Act (US Department of Labor, 1964), which made racial discrimination in public places such as theatres, restaurants and hotels illegal.

Some basic human rights were afforded in England through the Magna Carta of 1215, which established that neither the king nor his government was above the law but must be subject to it like other people. In 1932, a mass trespass took place on Kinder Scout in Derbyshire, protesting against members of the public being barred from having recreational access to Britain's mountains and moors. The landowners had sent their gamekeepers to defend their property, but they could not prevent the mass trespass. Members of the public do have a right to roam, and this is now enshrined in the *Countryside and Rights of Way Act 2000*. Safeguarding and protection have been important areas in the development of rights. The first piece of child protection legislation in England, known as the Children's Charter, came into effect in 1889. It enabled intervention by the authorities in families where a child was being ill-treated or subject to cruelty. A century later, the *Children Act 1989* was passed, introducing the paramountcy principle, which stated that the paramount consideration of the court in its decision making in childcare cases had to be the child's welfare (applied in the Charlie Gard case and discussed in Chapter 4). Another example concerned a 49 year-old man with autism who was non-verbal, had only limited understanding and lacked capacity to make decisions for himself. One day in 1997, while travelling to a day centre, he became agitated and was taken to Bournewood Hospital, a mental health facility where he remained for about three months. He had not been detained under the provisions of the *Mental Health Act 1983* but under a common law assumption of necessity. His carers, however, argued that he had been unlawfully detained. The British courts disagreed, but the ECHR ruled that under Article 5, his right to liberty had been violated. One problem arising from this case was the realisation that approximately 50,000 people were being cared for in secure care, or nursing homes and mental health hospitals under the same criteria. As a result, an amendment was made to the *Mental Capacity Act 2005* and the deprivation of liberty safeguards (DOLS) provision introduced (later amended to liberty protection safeguards, or LPS), which require a specific assessment of whether such detention is in the patient's best interest (Care Quality Commission, 2023). For a more detailed examination of this case, see Herring (2006, p 565).

Can the need for such rights be considered self-evident?

The need for many of these rights tends to crop up as the result of an individual or group being subject to unfair treatment but, importantly, at a point when either that individual or group decides to challenge their treatment. Their challenge has a better chance of succeeding if it coincides with the time when their claim is seen as just by others within the culture and the society in which they live. They are usually the result of a campaign, which is won or lost through being contested between those that have the power to grant them and those claiming them. However, this assertion can also be contested. In what may be regarded as one of the most significant statements ever made about the relationship between ruled and rulers – the *American Declaration of Independence* – the following was proclaimed in Congress on 4 July 1776:

We hold these truths to be self-evident, that all men are created equal, that they are endowed by their Creator with certain unalienable rights, that among these are Life, Liberty and the pursuit of Happiness. – That to secure these rights, Governments are instituted among Men, deriving their just powers from the consent of the governed.

These are fine words, but there is a fundamental flaw in these sentiments. What account was taken of the rights of the Indigenous people of America? Moreover, not including women rules out half of the people, and the number included was further reduced as the unalienable rights were available only to property-owning white men. Thomas Jefferson, a founding father of America and considered one of the principal authors of the Declaration was himself a slave owner, as were several others who, like him, achieved the office of president in the early years of independence. So it looks as though rights may be self-evident for members of the same socioeconomic group, race and gender, but when these characteristics are mixed, they seem far from self-evident and marginalised groups have often to fight for their own rights to be recognised. In 2024, there seems a way to go – for example, on 9 December 2023 John Burn-Murdock (2023) wrote an article in *The Financial Times* in which he referred to a study of the income equality of 18 countries in the developed world, revealing that the United States was the most unequal of them all.

Different sorts of rights

There are different sorts of rights and different contexts in which they may be claimed. One primary difference is where a right is a valid claim by those eligible, which obliges a response from those responsible to fulfil whatever the right enables the claimant to. For example, if you are an eligible child (currently or previously in the care of a local authority) that local authority, under their corporate parenting responsibilities, has a duty to carry out an assessment of your needs to determine what advice, assistance and support it would be appropriate for them to provide you with s *23(b) Children Act 1989*. These valid rights tend to be justified in accord with a set of rules, or specified in legislation, and are more than a claim – which may be weak or strong. These rights exist as something to which you are either entitled or not. For example, you have a right to vote in a general election provided you are not in prison and have reached the age of 18 years (Feinberg, in Banks, 2012, p 104). They often identify who is responsible for upholding the right, provide a remedy where the right has been violated and confer a degree of status, power and access to resources on the right-holder.

Compare this with rights that are emancipatory and aspirational in nature, often set out in manifestos or conventions; these are generally realised through advocacy and tend to be definitionally problematic and vague in identifying the body or individual responsible for meeting that right. For example, Article 28 of the United Nations Universal Declaration on the Rights of the Child, 1989 states that parties recognise the right of the child to education, with a view to achieving this right progressively and on the basis of equal opportunity. Although 196 countries are signatories to this declaration, there will be significant differences in the extent to which children are in receipt of education, with some being denied based on their gender. Article 2 protects children from discrimination of any kind. Afghanistan is a signatory to the convention, but reserved the right to express reservations on all provisions of the convention that are incompatible with the laws of Islamic Sharia law and local legislation in effect.

There are positive rights that can legitimately be claimed, provided you are eligible – for example, the right to medical treatment. There are negative rights, which often appear as liberties – freedoms to be able to do something without interference, although these are usually qualified. For example, in terms of freedom of speech, you are free to express an opinion; however, it is an offence if in so doing you incite hatred to an individual or group. Legal rights are those conferred through specific legislation. For example, you can apply to see certain information held about you under the provisions of the *Data Protection Act 1998*. There are moral rights, in which you can claim something, such as the right to be treated fairly. There are also rights that are absolute and applicable within a jurisdiction, without exception. Some rights may be limited – only applicable in certain circumstances – and others are conditional – subject to exceptions. Refer to the *Human Rights Act 1998* for more information.

In accordance with different rights, there are different contexts in which they might be applied. For example, employment law sets out the rights and responsibilities of employers and employees, and consumer laws sets out the rights and responsibilities for those selling and purchasing goods. An exception to rights appealing to specific interest groups is human rights, which are universally applicable to human beings within their mandated jurisdiction. For example, the *Human Rights Act 1998* is applicable to people in the United Kingdom. The *NHS Constitution* sets out the rights people have who use NHS services as a patient. It states that all healthcare staff should involve you (the patient) in decisions and treat you with kindness, dignity and respect. The rights specifically include:

- » access to health services;
- » good quality of care;
- » being treated by appropriately qualified and experienced staff;

» making decisions about medications and treatments;
» being protected from abuse and neglect;
» respect and confidentiality;
» making a complaint if you are not happy with your care or treatment or if things go wrong.

It also sets out target treatment waiting times for non-urgent procedures (18 weeks) and cancer diagnosis and treatment (two weeks) – although these are currently stretched due to increased pressures of demand.

Case study

Rights in contestation

On one level the application of rights may seem straightforward, where either a right for X to do Y exists or not. However, when their application is mixed with values a conflict can result. For example, the following describes an event that led to a level three complaint (needing to involve a local authorities' councillors in its resolution). It was customary practice for a day centre to hold a party at Christmas for its service users who had mild to moderate learning disabilities. A highlight of this party was when a local member of the rotary club (a charitable organisation that fundraisers for local good causes) would attend the centre dressed as Santa Claus and distribute presents to the service users, to their apparent delight. A newly appointed manager for learning disability learned of this 'customary practice' and cancelled the event, arguing it was patronising and paternalistic as the service users were adults and Santa Claus is a fairy story for young children. The more vocal service users made a complaint about the manager's decision which could not be resolved to the satisfaction of both sides without the involvement of the councillors, who authorised the private hiring of a hall in which to hold the party, complete with Santa's visit, which satisfied the service users. The fact that the premises did not belong to the local authority provided a face-saving measure for the manager. Who do you think best upheld the rights of those with learning disabilities?

A duty of care

This is an important concept that falls within the law of tort. Providers of certain services have a duty of care to those receiving these services where it is reasonably foreseeable that you could (potentially) cause injury or harm, through your actions or omissions, in providing that service. It is applicable to a wide range of professional relationships: teachers to their pupils; universities to their students; counsellors to their clients; social workers to their service users; and all health and social care practitioners to their patients. The duty that is owed includes promoting people's well-being and making sure they are safe from harm, abuse and injury. In situations considering whether the duty of care was breached, the law of negligence is usually applied, as discussed in Chapter 4 (Herring, 2006, p 40).

The duty of care is owed first and foremost to the practitioner's primary client. The extent to which it would be appropriate to extend it to secondary clients (carers, immediate family, parents) and tertiary clients (extended family, friends) needs careful consideration, especially where there is potential for conflict. For example, the doctors treating Charlie Gard (see Chapter 4) had a duty of care towards Charlie, but it would be difficult to extend it to his parents, who contested the decision to withdraw his treatment. Another example could arise in decisions about the care of elderly people. Imagine a scenario in which a patient, ready for discharge from hospital, had capacity and expressed a wish to return home. Physiotherapist and occupational therapy assessments had identified some risk that the patient acknowledged, but this had not deterred them from wanting to returning home. The patient's immediate family expressed a view that the risk was too great. Should health and social care staff support them and try to convince the patient that a care home is the appropriate option? No – the practitioner's primary client is the patient, and they should facilitate their patient's wishes and enable the patient's return home, minimising risk through the provision of aids and adaptations, fulfilling their duty of care and upholding the principle of autonomy. The duty of care can encompass the practitioner's obligation to uphold their client's rights. For example, a community care officer (CCO) visits Jack, a 74 year-old widower, to assess his eligibility for home care support to address some issues of alleged neglect made by his landlord, who visits while the CCO is undertaking their assessment. The landlord lists a number of areas where Jack is failing to take adequate care of himself and suggests it is time Jack went to a care home. Jack disagrees, and is adamant that he remains in his home. Jack has capacity and the CCO has a duty of care towards him. Jack has been in his tied cottage for a number of years and pays a very low rent. The landlord could charge a new tenant a much higher rent and the CCO suspects this may be part of the landlord's referral and suggestion that Jack goes into a care home. It is the CCO's responsibility to uphold Jack's right to remain at home provided he continues to fulfil his obligations as a tenant.

Rights and responsibilities: it's a two-way street

The rights discourse tends to be dominated by claims to rights, whether or not these are legitimate, often with rather less discussion about any corresponding responsibilities or obligations we may have towards that right being fulfilled. One might claim a right to well-being, health and happiness (although they do not exist in any meaningful way, as no one is identified to honour them) but the contribution the individual should make to help bring these desirable conditions about is a question that deserves serious consideration. One could argue that there is a moral responsibility on all of us to reduce the spread of infection, so if you knew you were infectious, you should comply with the government's advice and restrict contact with others – for example, during the Covid-19 pandemic or an influenza outbreak. Some of these responsibilities appear relatively straightforward: most of us would consider it wrong for a person diagnosed with AIDS to continue to have unprotected sex with partners who were ignorant of the diagnosis.

We know a degree of rationing takes place in the NHS due to demand outstripping the resources available, but whatever safeguards are put in place by bodies such as the National Institute for Health and Care Excellence (NICE) to try to ensure fair decisions are made in selecting the most efficacious treatments, the reality that some will receive treatment and others will not cannot be avoided. Some decisions may be at the policy level, but some will be clinical, and factors such as prospects for long-term recovery and benefit will be considered. But should the patient's lifestyle also be taken into account? We read in the previous chapter that in England 28 per cent of the population are obese, costing the NHS £6.1 billion, adding to the incidence of type 2 diabetes and causing joint problems in addition to cardiovascular and other issues. An eating disorder may be responsible for a proportion of this statistic but what if the cause is an unwillingness to limit the quantity of food consumed and improve the quality of their nutrition – should these patients have the same access to gastric band surgery or the drug Semaglutide as others? A similar argument could be made in the case of those with chronic respiratory problems if the patient continues to smoke. Such contentious debates could be applied to a variety of conditions, such as the association between poor mental health and substance misuse. So the question comes down to the extent to which we should be responsible for trying to maintain a good quality of health and well-being for ourselves. I will leave the reader to ponder on the possible answers.

Once rights have been established, is it job done?

This question prompts an image of the Jews, people with learning disabilities, homosexuals, communists and Romanies alighting from cattle trucks, having arrived at Auschwitz 80 years ago and systematically being stripped of any rights they had, with their destiny entirely at the whim of their captors. If this were an isolated example where human rights had been disregarded, we could perhaps condemn it to history; sadly, though, that is far from the case, as the testimony of organisations such as

Amnesty International bear out. Therefore, we must resist the rights we enjoy from becoming taken for granted and remain vigilant should they need defending. In many cases, they have been fought for and hard won, so each successive generation needs to establish their rights and strive to uphold them. In addition to maintaining established rights, we should also be alert to the need for adjustment to existing rights and argue for new ones in response to events as they unfold, as the following examples illustrate. It was not until 1992 that non-consensual sex (rape) between a married couple became illegal in the UK. Industrial disputes resulting in strike action cause disruption to the provision of some services – for example, health and transport. Within political discourse there is an argument calling for legislation to be introduced to ensure a level of essential service provision is maintained; if passed, it may be considered reasonable but could impact the workforce's right to strike.

Molly Russell was 14 years old when in 2017 she took her own life after viewing suicide and self-harm content online. Her father campaigned for legislation to compel internet platforms to take greater responsibility for the content uploaded to them and to empower Ofcom to hold them to account. This was realised through the Online Safety Bill, which became law in 2023. Also at the time of writing, traction has been secured after 20 years of campaigning for justice for over 900 postmasters wrongly accused of theft and fraud – and some of whom were even convicted – when the accounting errors were caused by a faulty computer system. The then prime minister Sunak has pledged to introduce legislation to exonerate them.

Martha Mills was 13 years old when she died of sepsis in hospital in 2021. Her parents had expressed increasing concerns about her deteriorating condition and questioned why she was not transferred to the intensive care unit (ICU). Her parents campaigned for a right to request a second medical opinion in situations of rapid deterioration of serious illness. In September 2023, the government announced its commitment to introduce what is dubbed Martha's Rule, enabling the right to a second opinion.

As we can see from the examples given here, it is difficult to envisage a time when the task of establishing rights to meet needs will be completed. As society changes, new situations develop, which give rise to new needs that require addressing. We must remain alert to the emergence of such needs in the continual quest to respond appropriately to them.

The development of human rights

As mentioned, one landmark in the development of the evolution of human rights was the Magna Carta of 1215. Other significant developments include the 1689 Bill of Rights (UK Parliament, 1689), the American Declaration of Independence 1776; the

French Declaration of the Rights of Man and Citizen 1789; The Universal Declaration of Human Rights, adopted by the United Nations General Council in 1948; the European Convention on Human Rights, 1950, ratified in 1953 and the creation of the European Court of Human Rights in 1959; and The Vienna Declaration and Programme of Action 1993, which resulted from the World Conference on Human Rights of the same year. However, perhaps the most significant of these in the modern era are the Universal Declaration of Human Rights 1948, which has 30 Articles, and the European Convention on Human Rights 1953. These conventions came about in response to World War II, to avoid a repetition of the atrocities and loss of life that occurred. The European Convention of Human Rights 1953 has 46 signatories and protects the rights of over 700 million people. It has over 59 articles, but only the first 18 relate to individual human rights. Many of them were incorporated into UK domestic law in 1998 through the *Human Rights Act*, which enabled claims of infringement of ECHR to be heard in British courts rather than having to lodge a hearing in the European Court of Human Rights in Strasbourg, although human rights cases can still be referred there if there is disagreement with the UK court's ruling. I used the term 'protecting the human rights' of the populations of the countries that are signatories, which is true given that if an individual thinks their human rights have not been upheld as entitled, there is a remedy through recourse to tribunals and courts. In itself, it does not protect the individual from infringement of their rights.

In the United Kingdom, we live under an unelected constitutional monarch, so people could be considered subjects rather than citizens. Monarchists think this arrangement is better than having an elected head or president, as in the case of the USA or France; however, republicans take the opposite view. Some counties have written constitutions, but the UK does not; perhaps the closest we have come to a bill of rights is the *Human Rights Act 1998*. The lack of a written constitution results in a negative response, in which there is a vague presumption that one may do something unless there is a law that expressly prohibits it. The position is clearer in countries such as America and Canada, where there is a written constitution based on a bill of rights laying out what rights are conferred on people and which freedoms and liberties the state will defend.

The UN Convention on the Rights of the Child

The United Nations Convention on the Rights of the Child 1989 contains 54 articles. Articles 1 to 41 address the civil, political, economic, cultural, health and educational rights of children. Articles 42 to 54 set out how the convention will be administered. A total of 197 countries have signed the convention, obliging states to refrain from acts that would defeat the convention's objectives and 196 have gone on to ratify it, which legally binds a state to implement the convention. The 196 include countries as disparate as Azerbaijan, Iran, India, Sweden and Somalia. The sole country that has signed but not yet ratified the convention is, perhaps surprisingly, the United States. The United Kingdom ratified it in 1991. However, as we saw in the paragraph on different sorts of rights, countries that have ratified it can also claim reservations on aspects of its implementation, due to incompatibility with existing law, culture or custom, adding to the reasons why the manifestation of its implementation differs so widely and why, for a significant number of children in the world, its objectives remain largely aspirational.

Article 1 defines a child as anyone under 18 years of age. Refer to the Convention for all 41 articles. There are four pillars of the CRC, which comprise Articles 2, 3, 6 and 12. Article 2 protects from discrimination, Article 3 states that the best interests of the child should be a primary consideration, Article 6 concerns the right to life and Article 12 states that a child's wishes and feelings should be heard in matters affecting them.

The United Kingdom demonstrates compliance with Article 12 through several tangible examples. The general one is the Gillick principle, discussed earlier. There are also numerous examples where a Local Authority's Children's Services are required by law to seek the views of the children for whom they are providing services. These may include support, safeguarding and being looked after. Where children are subject to civil court proceedings, their wishes and feelings have to be expressed in the court report (where they are of sufficient age and stage of maturity).

Article 12 is sufficiently specific to be able to determine the extent to which a party has implemented it. However, there are significant problems with definition in some articles, resulting in a lack of clarity about what a party should provide in order to be compliant. This can make the article appear aspirational in nature rather than setting standards and enforceable rights, and identifying the organs of state that could have responsibility for upholding them. For example, Article 23 talks of the right for children with disabilities to enjoy a full and decent life and Article 24 talks of the right of a child to enjoy the highest attainable standard of health. There is no definition of what constitutes a full and decent life or an acceptable standard of health. However, the UNCRC is the most widely ratified human rights treaty in history. Perhaps it would not be so had its authors been less accommodating of the existing law, culture and customs and the economic circumstances of its signatory states.

Monitoring progress?

The United Nations has a committee on the rights of the child which comprises 18 experts who monitor the implementation of the convention by its signatory states. These states are required to submit reports every five years to the UN committee, setting out the progress they have made on the implementation of the articles and optional protocols during the preceding five years. Evidence of infringement or lack of progress may attract critical comment through the UN committee's reports, but it cannot enforce compliance.

The *Human Rights Act 1998*

The *Human Rights Act 1998* and the *Equality Act 2010* have the status of statutory legislation as they are enshrined in domestic UK law. It is important to have an understanding of the development of human rights and the conventions that seek to establish them within their signatory states to gain an appreciation of your entitlements and responsibilities. I appreciate that many of the Articles introduced in this section do not have a direct bearing on health and social care, but an awareness of the rights these two pieces of legislation confer on UK citizens is necessary to enable you to know what you are entitled to and to fulfil your duty to uphold them for your fellow citizens.

The *Human Rights Act 1998* is a very important piece of legislation that incorporated many of the rights set out in the European Convention of Human Rights into UK domestic legislation in 2000. In its 2015 manifesto, the Conservative government pledged to introduce a Bill of Rights to repeal and replace the *Human Rights Act*, but this has not materialised despite Brexit. Many think it would be a bold, if not foolhardy government that would seek to deny any or change the rights of UK citizens to those enjoyed by over 700 million Europeans as recourse to the European Court of Human Rights would still be available (the United Kingdom remains a signatory to the Convention and as such has retained responsibilities to uphold it, despite Brexit). The articles and protocols in the *Human Rights Act 1998* contain social, economic, cultural, civil and political rights, the generic term for which is 'human rights'. There are 15 articles, but Articles 1, 13 and 15 are not incorporated from the Convention into the Act so the numbering runs from Articles 2 to 18. There are two protocols, the first and the sixth. Only four of the following Articles are absolute, meaning there are no circumstances in which legal derogation (deviation) may lawfully occur (see Article 3). The remainder may be limited, meaning the state can impose certain restrictions – for example, Article 12 limits the number of wives or husbands one may have at the same time, as polygamy (being married to more than one person at the same time) is not lawful in the United Kingdom. Alternatively, they may be conditional, meaning that the state can lawfully breach the right in specific circumstances (see Article 8). The 16 articles are as follows.

- » *Article 2: Right to life.* This article may be applied where a patient dies as a result of inadequate or incompetent medical care in which there is a case for arguing that the right was not upheld by the area health authority concerned and for which an Article 2 inquest may be held to determine the cause of death.

- » *Article 3: Prohibition of torture or inhuman or degrading treatment or punishment.* This article is absolute in that there are no circumstances in which you can be subject to torture, or inhuman or degrading treatment or punishment, within the jurisdiction of the United Kingdom.

- » *Article 4: Prohibition of slavery, servitude and forced or compulsory labour.* This is a limited article as there are circumstances in which it is lawful to request work to be undertaken – for example, in some institutions in which Article 5 may be lawfully infringed, such as detention in prison.

- » *Article 5: Right to liberty and security of the person.* This has to be a limited article, as there are numerous circumstances in which you may lawfully be denied your liberty, and it is not an infringement of this right. These include being subject to detention in prison, serving a sentence or on remand, in a secure hospital due to mental health, or a care or nursing home to prevent wandering if suffering impaired capacity through dementia, if there are grounds to arrest you, as part of investigating a crime, illegal immigration or prevention from spreading infectious diseases. However, all these procedures are subject to rules, regulations and laws so as to be compliant with Article 7. For example, involuntary detention in a secure mental health institution is governed by the *Mental Health Act 1983*.

- » *Article 6: Right to a fair trial.* This relates to both criminal and civil proceedings, and again is limited. Included is the presumption of innocence until proven guilty. There are limited circumstances in which a claim of an unfair trial might be upheld. For example, you cannot legitimately regard your trial as unfair because you were convicted, but you may have grounds to do so if important evidence was not submitted in your defence and was withheld unlawfully.

- » *Article 7: Prohibition of punishment without law.* This article prevents arbitrary punishment without due process of law. It also prohibits law being imposed retrospectively – that is, before your action was unlawful due to changes in the law or a heavier penalty being imposed due to changes in sentencing structure.

» *Article 8: Right to respect for privacy and family life, home and correspondence.* This is importantly a conditional right, the condition being: *'there shall be no interference by a public authority with the exercise of this right except such as is in accordance with the law and is necessary in a democratic society in the interests of national security, public safety or the economic well-being of the country, for the prevention of disorder or crime, for the protection of health or morals, or for the protection of the rights and freedoms of others'* (Human Rights Act 1998). This is a very important qualification, for you may assume that unless one of these conditions is met, there are no just grounds for a public body to interfere in your life unless you give your consent and thereby give your permission for it to do so. It is interesting to note that an absolute article can trump a conditional one if the condition is present, so if a child is suffering abuse at the hands of their carers (Article 3), the local authority's social services may intervene in lawful contravention of Article 8 as they would be protecting the rights of others – in this case, the child.

» *Article 9: Freedom of thought, conscience and religion.* This is a limited right: the first part upholds the right to opinion and belief but the second part, relating to religion, has implications not only to permit different religious beliefs but also regarding the extent to which reasonable manifestation and observance is facilitated. It is limited in what is prescribed by law and is necessary in a democratic society in the interests of public safety, for the protection of public order, health or morals, or for the protection of the rights and freedoms of others.

» *Article 10: Freedom of expression.* Clearly, this right distinguishes countries that have democratic governments from those that have totalitarian ones. However, it is a limited right as it carries certain duties and responsibilities, including the protection of the rights of others. This right does not entitle you to contravene the national laws and regulations so disclosing information received in confidence is not included in your freedom of expression, nor is an opinion designed to cause malicious offence, or incitement to hatred. (For the specific restrictions, see Article 10.2.)

» *Article 11: Freedom of assembly and association.* As with Article 10, this right is restricted to what is lawful (see Article 11.2 for the conditions). Police officers in the United Kingdom may join their Federation to protect their interests, but they are not allowed to take strike action because of the need for the maintenance of national security and law and order.

- *Article 12: Right to marry and found a family according to national laws.* This right is straightforward in that a nation's laws will prescribe who one may marry, at what age, the number of wives or husbands permitted and the official procedure to have the marriage recognised in law.

- *Article 14: Prohibition of discrimination in the enjoyment of rights and freedoms.* This wide-ranging right not to be discriminated against is perhaps best understood if it is restricted to the rights and freedoms in the Convention, including the various qualifications within the articles. So, while you may be a victim of discrimination in contravention of this right, you may have recourse to remedy provided you can prove it. Other national legislation may bolster this generic right with specific detail – for example, in the United Kingdom, the *Equality Act 2010*.

- *Article 16: Restrictions on political activity of non-nationals.* A signatory country may impose certain restrictions on the political activity of its non-national population without being in contravention of Articles, 10, 11 and 14. We might assume these measures would apply if the 'political activity' was regarded as posing a threat to the host nation or its nationals, as could be the case with insurrection or terrorism.

- *Article 17: Prohibition of the abuse of rights.* This concerns the protection of the integrity of the rights and freedoms set out in the Convention.

- *Article 18: Limitation on use of restrictions on rights.* This is similar to Article 17 in that it is to protect the spirit of the Convention and guard against the rights and freedoms provided for within it to be distorted or undermined.

The first protocol (protocol meaning rule or procedure):

- *Article 1: Right to peaceful enjoyment of possessions.* This makes exceptions for international and national laws and regulations, such as a government's power to impose taxes.

- *Article 2: Right to education.* This article has the potential to be quite contentious where the nation-state's education system is secular or where the children's wishes could conflict with those of their parents. It also has the potential to be contentious in educational provision where a school exerts the right to exclude a child and for children with non-mainstream needs.

- *Article 3: Right to free elections.* Elections to governments should be held freely and fairly.

The sixth protocol:

- » *Article 1: Abolition of the death penalty.* Judiciaries cannot impose the death penalty as a sentence.
- » *Article 2: Death penalty in time of war.* This permits derogation of Article 1 in this protocol in times of war or the threat of war.

The *Human Rights Act 1998* is essentially the adoption of the European Convention on Human Rights into UK domestic legislation. The Convention is, to its supporters, a triumph of the application of modernism, as discussed in Chapter 3, in that universal principles and values can be established and their application striven for. Critics of the Convention may point to its failings, or perhaps more precisely where human behaviour has not lived up to its aspirations. However, it is worth remembering that the extent to which we may enjoy the rights and freedoms afforded to us by the Convention is directly proportional to the extent to which we are willing to uphold the rights and freedoms it confers on others. Furthermore, realisation of the rights and freedoms requires the organs of the state to function with probity, free of corruption and nepotism, and ideally where there is some independence between the judiciary, executive (government) and police. The existence of a free press to hold these bodies to account acts as an important safeguard.

The *Equality Act 2010*

The *Equality Act 2010* builds on the platform created by Article 14 of the HRA, 1998 and makes it unlawful to discriminate against anyone in the United Kingdom on the grounds of nine 'protected characteristics':

1. age;
2. being or becoming a transgender person;
3. being married or in a civil partnership;
4. being pregnant or on maternity leave;
5. being disabled;
6. race, including colour, nationality, ethnic or national origin;
7. religion, belief or lack of religion/belief;
8. sex (includes cis, inter, and non-gendered);
9. sexual orientation.

You are also protected if you are with another person who has a protected characteristic, such as a family member or friend, or if you have complained about discrimination or supported someone else's claim. This does not prevent anyone in the United Kingdom being subject to discrimination on these grounds but does provide for legal remedy if you can demonstrate you have been. The situation in which these protections apply are:

- at work;
- in education;
- as a consumer;
- when using public services;
- when buying or renting property;
- as a member or guest of a private club or association.

Under the *Equality Act 2010*, there are four types of discrimination.

1. *Direct discrimination: treating one person worse than another.* For example, a team leader is aware that an opportunity for promotion in her team is coming up and informs those she thinks could do a good job. She does not include one member because she knows she is trying for a baby and does not want the new post-holder to be going on maternity leave.

2. *Indirect discrimination: organisational policy or procedure that has a worse impact on someone with a protected characteristic.* However, this does not have to be a policy, it could be a rule or just a way of doing something. For example, your health centre is running a public health campaign on awareness-raising for women approaching the menopause. The five sessions are scheduled to run from 9am until 10.30am on Wednesdays. There is no rolling programme proposed at different times or on a different day, which disadvantages working women and those with childcare responsibilities.

3. *Harassment: treatment that violates dignity or creates a hostile, degrading, humiliating or offensive environment.* For example, you are out on a social evening looking after a small group of people with learning difficulties and you visit a pub. You become aware of a customer making derogatory comments about your group and saying they should not be allowed to attend an ordinary pub.

4. *Victimisation: treatment that disadvantages someone and is unfair because they make a claim under the* Equality Act 2010 *or someone who is supporting someone doing so.* For example, an employee makes a complaint of sexual harassment at work and is dismissed as a consequence.

An example of direct discrimination concerned Liverpool senior nurse, Michelle Cox, who won a landmark case against NHS England Improvement after the court heard evidence of her harassment and victimisation by her employer. Furthermore, her whistleblowing claims were disregarded after she raised a grievance and an appeal.

The employment tribunal found that Ms Cox's manager, Gill Pax, sidelined, undermined and intimidated her. Direct discrimination took the form of purposefully excluding Ms Cox from team away days and Pax excluding her from recruiting to new senior posts in her team. These are two examples of several occasions of direct discrimination suffered by Ms Cox. The tribunal found that Ms Cox was a victim of a 'hostile and humiliating environment'. The Royal College of Nursing supported her, and she is in line to secure substantial compensation after being dismissed and discredited by her manager between 2019 and 2021 (Mangion, 2024).

There are situations where groups of people are treated differently but in a manner that has a rationale and can be justified, so it is not regarded as direct or indirect discrimination. For example, the NHS offers bowel cancer screening to people aged 60–74 years. This age range is selected based on increased incidence, not preferential treatment.

As an academic and someone interested in the development of rights, I regarded the failure to include class as a protected characteristic a significant omission that will need to be addressed in the future. Further examples of direct and indirect discrimination can be found on the Equality and Human Rights Commission website (www.equalityhumanrights.com) (EHRC, 2019).

The distinction between positive discrimination and positive action

The *Equality Act 2010* draws a distinction between positive action, which is permitted in the legislation, and positive discrimination, which is not. Positive action is where, for example, a student course might be advertised as 'applications from BME [Black and minority ethnic] or female candidates are welcome', acting as an encouragement to address disproportional representation in the candidature – for example, in engineering. This type of positive action is legal and is not an infringement of the *Equality Act 2010*. However, if the admissions tutor interviewing the candidates for a place on the engineering course used a lower threshold for BME or female candidates than for other candidates, this would constitute positive discrimination, which is illegal and would contravene the *Equality Act 2010* because it would be subjecting non-BME and male candidates to direct discrimination.

Public bodies and service providers are required to make 'reasonable adjustments' to enable people with disabilities to participate and avoid unlawfully discriminating against people with a disability. Examples could include providing access for differences in mobility, such as a bridge with a lift as well as steps, or the provision of learning support plans for those with dyslexia.

Discrimination

Some discussion about discrimination in general terms has taken place earlier in this book but, given that the potential for the discriminatory treatment of others is ever-present, it is worth revisiting. Choosing one thing over another – in other words, expressing a preference for something – is an act of discrimination in that a distinction is made, a differentiation. There are other examples in which certain individuals or groups are excluded from entering or participating in particular activities and opportunities, which is also an act of discrimination. Consider the entry requirements for studying for a degree in health and social care, which will include age – usually 18 years – and qualification gates, such as GCSEs, which permit those eligible to apply and prevent those who are not. However, there are sound reasons for the exercise of such discrimination, such as maintaining the credibility of qualifying credentials for entry into certain professions. There are exceptions – albeit rare – to the *Equality Act 2010* to allow for the restriction of applicants for certain jobs in specific circumstances – for example, female-only applicants for a job in a women's refuge. This would be considered a genuine occupational qualification, and any advertising for the post would need to specify this. Such discrimination is reasonable and lawful because of the rationale used to justify it. The discrimination considered unlawful and offensive is that resulting in unjust, unfair treatment, which makes the recipient less equal in their value and worth in the eyes of those discriminating against them. In fact, regarding someone as equal to yourself in terms of their value and worth as a human being helps to safeguard them from unjust or unfair discrimination as it is very difficult to discriminate against them if you regard them as an equal. There may be a moral argument for regarding one's fellow human beings as equal but doing so strengthens their case for comparable access to goods, services and resources.

It is one thing to consider this on a national scale but extending it to international or even global levels is quite disturbing, given the extent of inequality we see. One way of minimising this discomforting thought, or cognitive dissonance, is to tacitly regard inequality as somehow deserved, coming to regard those without as being lazy and feckless or, for those with, bestowed on more industrious peoples, rather than simply being fortunate in the time and place of one's birth, or a mix of the two. So, perhaps discrimination is endemic in human society, but is it inevitable? In the United Kingdom, we have seen a seismic change over 40 years in both attitude and law towards those seeking or in relationships with people of the same sex, but we remain vulnerable to intolerance, and progress in addressing it takes time if it occurs at all. So how easy is it to create discrimination? How long does it take?

Answers to these questions were provided through an innovative exercise to which a primary school teacher named Jane Elliot in Riceville, Ohio subjected her class in the 1960s. She wanted to address racism and devised an experiment in which she divided her class not by skin colour, as all the children were white, but by eye colour. She made brown and blue bibs for the children to wear, indicating their eye colour from a distance. She then told the class that the blue-eyed people were better, smarter and tidier, and that this would be rewarded by privileges such as being allowed to use the playground equipment and enjoying a second helping of food at lunch; those with brown eyes would not enjoy these privileges. By mid-morning break on the first day, the children had segregated into association by eye colour, disrupting established friendships. The blue-eyed children appeared buoyant, enjoying their new-found status; the brown-eyed children were downcast and miserable. Two of the boys had a fight, which started when one called the other a browneye. A new term of abuse had been created and in less than a day Jane Elliot had created a microcosm of society in her classroom. The next day, Jane Elliot shocked her class by saying that yesterday she had lied (herself being blue eyed) and that the truth was that brown-eyed people were in fact the better, smarter group. She then reversed the privileges. Later that day, she brought the class together again in celebration of their individual talents, destroying the bibs and flip-flopped superiority/inferiority she had so easily created. There were some ethical issues in subjecting her children to this, as she was in a position of trust. If not handled competently, it could have been damaging; however, she felt that inducing the lived experience of being discriminated against and discriminating was worth it. The exercise, which she repeated with her class over several years, became the subject of a documentary known as *A Class Divided or The Eye of the Storm* and its video is well worth watching (see www.pbs.org/video/frontline-class-divided).

Discrimination can be understood as the differential treatment of a person or group, especially in a worse way, based on a particular characteristic. Oppression is caused when being subject to harsh and cruel treatment, but also occurs when discrimination is institutionalised, and individuals or groups are governed in an unfair and unjust way that impacts their opportunities and freedoms. The ideas used to justify and maintain or promote discrimination and oppression can be represented in ideology – for example, institutional racism is an ideology that suggests people of a certain ethnic origin are not as capable of undertaking or worthy of certain roles or outcomes compared with other ethnicities.

For example, the MacPherson Inquiry into the death of Black teenager Stephen Lawrence found the Metropolitan Police Force to be institutionally racist (MacPherson Inquiry, 1999). Other means of transmitting discrimination and oppression include through hegemony, or the dominant ideas of the time in society – what is considered given, or the way things are, giving rise to social norms and language. We have a rich vocabulary available to us, but the words we use can both reflect and construct discrimination, causing exclusion and invisibility – for example, failing to acknowledge women, as in the use of the word 'mankind' or dehumanising and depersonalising terms such as 'invalid' and 'the elderly'. Political correctness has been criticised for being oppressive, yet it has sought to encourage the sensitive use of language to avoid causing offence. All these ideas have one thing in common: they rely on an us-and-them concept and terminology based on difference.

In itself, the recognition of difference is not discriminatory. Indeed, as human beings, we are psychologically attuned to recognise difference very quickly, as we may need a flight-or-fight response for our survival. However, our response to difference can be discriminatory and can elicit a range of reactions, from being unhelpful in enabling us get along with our fellow humans to committing hate crimes against them.

Exercise

Think of a group that is different from that to which you consider you belong.

» How do you see difference in relation to the following descriptions?

   a) As a threat, which you might see as dangerous or deficient, prompting closed and defensive practice?

   b) As an opportunity, enriching diversity, prompting open practice and curiosity?

   c) Another response?

We can think of our response to diversity as being on a continuum, within a range from recognition, where the issue is barely tolerated, to a celebration of it. For example, not all manifestations of diversity are worthy of respect. My values dictate that I regard the Taliban's treatment of women in Afghanistan as oppressive, and therefore cannot respect the beliefs that underpin it. However, I give recognition to them insofar as they are a fact, they exist and it may be some time before Afghani women will again enjoy the human rights and freedoms that many other women do. If we promote LGBTQ+ rights or define ourselves as such, we might celebrate a gay pride event. It is possible that a discriminatory response is so extreme that its manifestation is denied, not recognised, and ultimately not tolerated, resulting in a hate crime. The Labour MP Jo Cox, who held liberal views about immigration and asylum seekers, was murdered in June 2016 by Thomas Mair, who held far-right political views that were so diametrically opposed to Jo's; he apparently could not accept that she had a legitimate right to expression and could not tolerate her continued existence.

Consider the diagram in Figure 5.1. You will see that a neutral response to an issue of diversity is acknowledgement. Positioning yourself here on an issue of difference implies that you acknowledge the phenomenon but do not have a strong reaction to it, either in support of or against it. If you positioned yourself at the point of valuing it, you would feel that it was beneficial and would be shifted towards the non-discriminatory end of the continuum, whereas if you were critical of the issue, you would be shifted towards the discriminatory end. For example, let's consider the issue of immigration into the United Kingdom. If you value this, you would be likely to think it adds richness and diversity to our culture, fulfilling many jobs the local workforce is unwilling to do and contributing to the economy. If you were critical, you might think the United Kingdom sufficiently populated and unable to support increasing numbers, with access to public services and housing stretched as it is. Or you might differentiate between an obligation to provide asylum for genuine asylum seekers against economic immigrants, supporting the former and being critical of the latter.

A useful model was developed by trainer and writer Neil Thompson. It is known as the PCS model, where P stands for personal/psychological and concerns the individual's thoughts, feelings and actions; C stands for cultural, and concerns shared ways

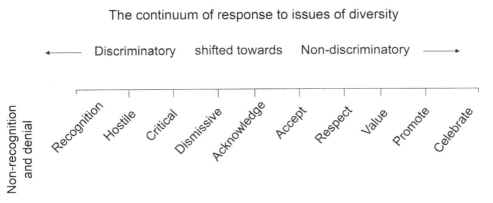

Figure 5.1 Continuum diversity model

> ### Exercise
>
> Identify an issue of diversity that you support and one you do not support. Consider where on the continuum in Figure 5.1 you would position your responses. Now analyse your reasons for so doing, identifying what influenced your decision. It is an interesting exercise to then consider the merits of the opposing view. You might think it does not have any – this view condemns you to a 'I'm right and they are wrong' dynamic, whereas if you can find any merit in the opposing view, you are taking a different perspective, which can promote a greater degree of tolerance towards difference.

of seeing things, thinking and doing; and S stands for structural, and concerns institutionalised norms that are sewn into the fabric of society (Thompson, 2006). The three levels in the model are interconnected, and can influence and support each other.

For example, not so long ago, if you were a wheelchair user it was not uncommon to find access to some buildings and facilities barred to you as there were no lifts or ramps by which to gain entry. At the time, it seemed generally acceptable that this was the case, so at a personal level one became accustomed to not seeing people with disability taking up fully participatory roles in society, and this was viewed as a consequence of their disability. This was reflected at a cultural level in much of the local community: facilities such as programmes with a sign language option were rare, as were traffic crossings with a beeping noise permitting crossing as well as a visual signal. Walkways with lowered kerbs for wheelchair users or dimpled paving to allow the blind knowledge of a crossing were absent. At a structural level, some legislation did exist for people with disability, and the welfare state recognised a need for financial support through payments such as attendance allowance so people could be attended to at home.

However, maintaining this oppressive status quo became unacceptable to the disability rights movement, which protested in the late 1970s and 1980s, effectively bringing about change at the personal, cultural and structural levels. People with disabilities play a far more participatory role in society today, and are represented in employment, sport, politics and broadcasting. Their increased visibility creates the new normal. At a cultural level, we see disabled sportspeople competing in the Paralympics and Invictus Games. At a structural level, a personal budget may be applied to enable people with disabilities to employ their carers and have more control over how the money is spent. Through the *Equality Act 2010*, disability is a protected characteristic allowing for reasonable adjustment to be made, enabling participation and ending unlawful discrimination on the grounds of disability. These changes brought about a new paradigm in thinking about disability; it was not caused by the nature of the disability itself, but rather the lack of facilities in society to enable participation.

Thompson makes a distinction between non-discriminatory practice and anti-discriminatory practice, with the former being practice absent of discrimination and the latter being where the practitioner takes a proactive approach to combat discrimination. For example, while you are out enjoying a social event in a pub, someone in your group makes a sexist and misogynistic comment as a joke about a woman's appearance. You go along with it and laugh, avoiding what might otherwise be an awkward moment. This is discriminatory, as you are joining in with the discrimination. The same thing occurs but this time you don't laugh or respond; this would be non-discriminatory because you are not joining in with it. If you challenge the comment, this would be anti-discriminatory as you are doing something positive to combat discrimination.

Navigating discrimination: a personal approach

Finding your own ethical pathway through the terrain of discrimination is a complex and demanding task. It would be easy to deny the contribution we make to discrimination, but this would be simplistic and run the risk of being dishonest. The phrase 'hell is other people' is famously attributed to the French philosopher Jean Paul Sartre. I don't believe this was simply an expression of dislike of others, but rather an acknowledgement that other people constantly present us with difference, often challenging our perception of how we would like the world to be. Again, it would be easy to say that I celebrate all manifestations of diversity, but this would suffer from similar problems to the claim of not discriminating.

One approach I have found helpful in navigating an acceptable pathway through what I have described as the terrain of discrimination is to apply a rule of thumb measure about what we can be reasonably held responsible for and what we cannot. Let me explain: as a White male if I thought myself to be a higher order of being than people of colour or women, I would be a white supremacist or a misogynist. I find such ideas abhorrent, but if I did hold them I would be responsible for choosing to hold such opinions, inviting critical censure from those who regard such views as abhorrent. However, we also have characteristics for which we cannot reasonably be held responsible. An example is our skin colour – or, more accurately, the amount of melanin in our skin, which is determined by the latitude at which your forebears lived and the degree of exposure to sunlight. The greater the degree of exposure to ultraviolet radiation, the more melanin is required in your skin to protect you against it. We do not choose our skin colour any more than we choose our date of birth – or eye colour, in reference to Jane Elliot's exercise. These are known as essentialist characteristics – those that are essential to us. We are not culpable for these characteristics so it would be wrong to discriminate against people for these, unlike some opinions people hold – for example, against human rights.

Conclusion

In this wide-ranging chapter, several characteristics of rights have been considered, including the meaning of a right, how the need for a right is recognised and whether this is self-evident, different sorts of rights, our responsibilities in enjoying entitlement to rights and, once established, whether they are safe. The development of human rights was explored before the *Human Rights Act 1998* and the *Equality Act 2010* were introduced. Finally, the issue of discrimination was revisited, contextualised in the light of this legislation, and a personal approach to navigating this complex but important aspect of human relations was offered for the reader's consideration.

Chapter 6 | Consent and confidentiality

This chapter considers the important issues of consent and confidentiality, and looks at the significance of their application within health and social care.

Consent

It is both a legal and ethical requirement that health and social care practitioners obtain their competent client's or patient's consent before any treatment is undertaken. Failure to do so could result in a criminal offence, namely battery, or trespass to the person or negligence. The sorts of things for which obtaining consent is required include:

- » a physical examination;
- » surgical procedures;
- » undertaking an assessment;
- » providing social care services;
- » a blood test;
- » providing day care services;
- » undergoing chemotherapy;
- » participating in an educational or social activity provided as part of a care package.

There are several reasons why obtaining consent is so important:

- » autonomy is the overriding principle of medical ethics;
- » it protects the client's or patient's dignity;
- » it avoids paternalism;
- » it enables trust;
- » the service user is more likely to agree to an intervention if they have been involved in the choice;
- » it is a legal requirement;
- » it protects the practitioner.

Consent may be given in a variety of ways, according to the degree of invasiveness of the proposed procedure. It may be implied, for example, when the GP says to the patient, 'I'm just going to check your blood pressure,' where the patient rolls up their sleeve of their arm in readiness for the cuff. It may be oral, for example, where the nurse says, 'I'm just going to take your temperature by placing this probe in your ear – it that alright?' and the patient agrees. Written consent needs to be obtained for more invasive procedures such as surgery. For the caregiver to have implied or oral consent, they must be satisfied that the patient or client understands the purpose of the intervention and why it has been suggested.

For consent to be valid, it must be voluntary and informed. Informed consent is more than simply gaining agreement. It includes a description of what the procedure or process involves, anticipated outcomes, any risks or side-effects, likely consequences of the procedure or process not being undertaken, alternatives to the proposed procedure or process and any anticipated outcomes, risks or side-effects. This enables the client or patient to make an informed decision, after weighing up the options, their benefits and the consequences.

How do you know whether the consent given is genuine and they have understood what you have said? You can check this by asking the client or patient, after you have given the information that enables their consent to be informed, about their understanding of the proposed procedure, its benefits and its effects. If you are confident that the client or patient has understood what the proposed procedure involves and are therefore able to make an informed decision you may proceed; if they withhold their consent, you must abide by their decision, even if you do not agree or you think they have made a poor or bad choice.

There are potential challenges to expressions of consent, which include the following.

- » The patient may feel coerced by professionals, partners or relatives. This can be checked out by asking the client or patient if they feel under any pressure to agree to the procedure.
- » They may feel impeded or restrained by information or time. This can be nullified by asking the client or patient if they have any questions.
- » They may not have the capacity to understand. There can be a variety of reasons, which may range from communication issues – for example, where different languages are involved – to a lack of capacity – for example, due to dementia.

At the beginning of this section on consent, the word 'competent' was used to qualify who can give their consent. There are several circumstances where the patient's or client's competence to give their consent is compromised or unavailable. Some of these circumstances are discussed below.

Mental capacity and people who lack capacity

Under the provisions of the *Mental Capacity Act 2005*, a person must be deemed to have capacity unless it is proven that they do not. The proof is determined by assessment in a two-stage test that must comply with the code of practice for such assessments under the *Mental Capacity Act 2005*. Authority to undertake these assessments requires specific training. There are five principles that must be followed when assessing capacity:

1. There is a presumption that a person has capacity unless proven otherwise.
2. Individuals should be supported to maximise their own decision-making.
3. Unwise decisions cannot be seen as wrong decisions.
4. Decisions made on behalf of someone lacking capacity must be made in their best interests (efforts must be made to establish this; where advance directives do not exist, consultation with family and friends can provide an indication of what the person concerned may have wanted to happen).
5. Any decision made on behalf of someone who lacks capacity must be made in such a way as to be least restrictive on the person's rights and freedoms.

These principles do not apply solely to medical decisions; they impact any decision affecting the person's life, such as financial and social decisions.

The types of circumstances in which decisions may have to be made on behalf of someone include as a result of:

- stroke;
- brain injury;
- mental health problems;
- dementia;
- learning disability;
- confusion, drowsiness caused by illness or treatment;
- substance misuse;
- anaesthesia, sedation or induced coma.

Advance directives and power of attorney

Where the patient has made an advance directive (*Mental Capacity Act 2005* s 24), also known as a living will, it should contain information about what the person concerned is willing to give their consent to and what they would not, and these wishes should be upheld. The patient may also have created a lasting power of attorney (*Mental Capacity Act 2005* s 9); if so, the person identified as being so entrusted may make the decision. In some situations, a court may have appointed a deputy (*Mental Capacity Act 2005* s 16) who can make a decision on behalf of the person for whom they are deputising. It is also possible to identify a surrogate or consenting proxy in advance, who may be a personal consultee, a family member or close friend, or a professional person who can advise on what the person's wishes might be. Section 35 of the *Mental Capacity Act 2005* makes provision for the creation of independent mental capacity advocates who may be consulted on cases where decision-making is solely limited to a medical professional. In situations where a lack of capacity is likely to be temporary, any decisions made on that person's behalf should only be made as necessary, and those that can await the person's return to capacity should be delayed. Where the person is deemed to lack capacity due to mental health problems, certain provisions under the *Mental Health Act 1983* can permit treatment, overriding the requirement to obtain the patient's consent.

There may be medical emergencies in which action needs to be taken without having obtained consent – for example, a medic attending the scene of an accident in which the patient is unconscious. It would, of course, be unacceptable not to treat the victim of the accident due to a lack of consent, due to the overriding principle to preserve life. In such situations, the defence of necessity applies. There are also situations of uncertainly regarding how best to proceed. For example, a surgeon undertaking a routine operation discovers what is suspected to be a malignant growth. The surgeon has obtained consent for the routine procedure, but not for anything else. Should they excise the growth to avoid another operation, despite not having consent to do so? Perhaps this could be defended under the principle of necessity if the procedure could be considered lifesaving or where not proceeding could endanger the patient's life. This would constitute an emergency waiver of consent. The surgeon might opt for a safer route and take a biopsy only. Finally, there are circumstances in which the treatment/consent decision pose especially difficult ethical and legal issues. For example, prisoners on hunger strike, or some eating disorders with life-threatening consequences. Should such people be force-fed or left to die? In such matters, the principle of preserving life clashes with that of autonomy unless impairment or lack of capacity can be proven. In such cases, recourse to legal rulings may be appropriate.

Children, young people and consent

The *Mental Capacity Act* 2005 only applies to people who are 16 years of age and over. Young people aged 16 and over can give their own consent; under the *Mental Capacity Act* 2005, they are automatically deemed to have capacity, unless proven otherwise. Children under 16 can give their consent provided they are deemed to be Gillick competent (see Chapter 4), which means being capable of reasoned, informed decision-making. A young child, or a child not considered Gillick competent, cannot give their consent but adults holding parental responsibility for the child can give consent on their behalf, unless it can be proven that they lack the capacity to do so. There can be circumstances in which a competent adult with parental responsibility for a child unable to give their own consent denies the child treatment or requests that the child receives treatment that the medics do not consider is in the child's best interest. In such disputes, the court of protection can rule in favour of or against the parties' petition, as we saw with the Charlie Gard case in Chapter 4.

Case study

Children and consent

To illustrate how seriously the issue of consent is regarded, consider the case of Hannah Jones, who in 2008 was 13 years old and suffering heart failure, thought to be exacerbated by chemotherapy used to treat her leukaemia. She had been ill for so long that she was inclined not to give her consent for the heart transplant her doctors wished her to have, despite its potential to be a life-saving and necessary treatment. The hospital initially instigated legal proceedings with a view to obtain a ruling that the need for her consent be waived so the procedure could go ahead. However, the safeguarding officer from the hospital interviewed Hannah without her parents and deemed her not subject to undue influence and Gillick competent, and the hospital withdrew its application. Eight months later, Hannah changed her mind and gave her consent for the transplant. She recently graduated from university. The case shows how the rights of the child, through Gillick competency, can hold sway even in such serious circumstances and how a change of mind may take place at any point in the consent process.

This section on consent provides a brief introduction to some of the main ideas underpinning this important topic in medical ethics and human rights. Many of the day-to-day decisions regarding consent are relatively straightforward, and clinicians might not need to get to grips with the many stated cases that have given rulings and subsequent guidance in complex situations. However, health and social care practitioners do need to acquaint themselves with and abide by their employer's guidance, policy and procedure on consent, in addition to service-specific guidance (see NHS, 2022; Care Quality Commission, 2011).

Confidentiality

Equivalent to the importance attached to consent is that of confidentiality, and practitioners should manage the information to which they have access in the course of their work lawfully, competently and in compliance with the information governance directives of their employer. Recent developments of the proliferation of social media and the introduction of the General Data Protection Regulation have added to the complexity of managing information appropriately.

A useful starting point for those who, in the course of their work, gain access to information on or about other people is to regard such information as privileged. Doing so may prompt the recipient to take care of the information they possess. Another useful idea is to remember that information is not solely what we know about a client or a patient, their personal details, information about their condition and so on; it also includes what we, as practitioners, add to through the maintenance of good reporting and recording. Furthermore, it is important to be mindful of the likelihood that the client or the patient exerts their right to see what is written about them, so write your comments as if they are looking over your shoulder as you write. Depending on the type of assessment being made – for example, of the quality of care being provided by a carer to a child or vulnerable person – being aware that what you write may be read by the person concerned does not imply any concern should be watered down or any comment otherwise considered relevant should be omitted. However, what is written should be accurate, balanced and lawful, should distinguish between fact, opinion and hearsay, and should be devoid of unlawful discrimination. If what is written contains contributions from others, you should obtain their consent before it is shared with the person concerned.

Herring (2006, p 145) asserts that managing information properly is more than obliging staff to avoid unnecessary or unlawful breaches of their clients' or patients' confidential information. Organisations must take positive measures to ensure the confidential information they hold is held lawfully and not revealed.

This includes ensuring information, both on paper and electronically, is held securely, that reasonable steps have been taken to protect it from hacking, theft or being lost, or being seen by those not eligible to read it. Also, it needs to be held in accordance with specified timescales and, thereafter, destroyed appropriately. This involves maintaining tidy workstations, having strong and secure log-on passwords, enforced rules about what information may be removed from the designated workstation by staff or students, and procedures for its protection, and to whom any loss or theft should be reported.

Data protection is governed principally by two pieces of legislation: the *Data Protection Act 1998* and the *Data Protection Act 2018*.

The *Data Protection Act 1998*

This Act cites eight principles that must be adhered to:

1. Data must be handled fairly and lawfully.
2. Personal data must be obtained and processed for specific and lawful purposes, which are compatible with those for which it was obtained.
3. Data obtained must be adequate, relevant and not excessive.
4. It must be accurate and up to date.
5. It must not be kept for longer than is necessary.
6. The subject has a right to access information held about them.
7. It must be protected by appropriate security.
8. It should not be transferred outside the European Economic Area without checks being made.

Some of these principles are repeated in a more recent piece of legislation, the *Data Protection Act 2018*, which was introduced to incorporate the General Data Protection Regulation 2018 into UK domestic legislation. It includes the following principles:

» Everyone responsible for using someone's personal data must ensure it is used fairly, lawfully and transparently.
» It is only used for specified, explicit purposes.
» It is used in a way that is adequate, relevant and limited to only what is necessary.
» It is accurate and, where necessary, kept up to date.
» It is kept for no longer than necessary.
» It is handled in a way that ensures appropriate security, including protection against unlawful or unauthorised processing, access, loss, destruction or damage.

The General Data Protection Regulation 2018 makes provision for stronger legal protection for more sensitive information on such matters as:

- race;
- ethnic background;
- political opinions;
- religious beliefs;
- trade union membership;
- genetics;
- biometrics (where used for identification);
- health;
- sex life or orientation.

There are separate safeguards for personal data relating to criminal convictions and offences.

Under the *Data Protection Act 2018*, you have the right to find out what information the government and other organisations store about you. These include the right to:

- be informed about how your data is being used;
- access personal data;
- have incorrect data updated;
- have data erased;
- stop or restrict the processing of your data;
- data portability (allowing you to get and reuse your data for different services);
- object to how your data are processed in certain circumstances.

You also have rights when an organisation is using your personal data for:

- automated decision-making processes (without human involvement);
- profiling – for example to predict your behaviour or interests.

For further detail, you can view that Acts themselves on the UK Government website at www.legislation.gov.uk.

In 1997, Dame Fiona Caldicott chaired a committee to report on confidentiality, out of which were established eight principles for safely handling people's personal data. These are known as the Caldicott principles.

1. Justify the purpose for needing the information.
2. Use confidential information about someone only when necessary and for the purpose for which it was obtained.
3. Use only the minimum information necessary to fulfil the task for which it was obtained.
4. Come to know the information and share it on a strictly need-to-know basis.
5. Be aware of your responsibilities when handling confidential information.
6. Comply with the law.
7. Health and social care professionals have a duty to share information to facilitate appropriate individual care and this duty is as important as the duty to protect patient confidentiality.
8. Inform the patient or service user about how their confidential information is used, including who it might be shared with.

Some organisations appoint a Caldicott Guardian to advise on novel or especially complex situations in respect of confidentiality.

No breach of confidence or a breach has a legitimate defence

There is no breach of confidence where you have the consent of the person whose information is to be shared; however, what is to be shared and with whom needs to be agreed. For example, a patient might ask their doctor to share details of their condition and prognosis with their partner.

There may be specific circumstances where information is not of a confidential nature, as may be the case with information considered trivial, such as a preference for tea over coffee, or where the information is no longer confidential because it has become public knowledge. However, such situations can be subject to dispute and assumptions should not be made but instead checked out.

You might consider that you are not breaching confidence because you have protected the identity of the person concerned though removing or changing their name in the records. However, you need to be sure that the person's identity cannot be worked out by those who know the workplace and can second-guess the person's identity through details of an event or circumstances.

There are some situations in which a breach of confidentiality can be justified and legitimately defended. These include when it can be argued that it is in the public interest to do so. For example, during a mental health assessment, a patient discloses an intention to harm themselves or others. It may be considered in the public interest to breach the patient's confidence to prevent harm. However, organisations can find themselves on the wrong side of proceedings brought in public-interest cases. For example, the BBC argued that its coverage of the police raid on the home of Sir Cliff Richard in 2014 was a matter of public interest due to his celebrity status. However, the judge found in favour of Sir Cliff because news reports had violated his privacy and breached the *Data Protection Act 1998* and a large claim for compensation was ordered against the BBC.

Imagine a large, busy hospital with several departments and a patient having appointments in a number of these for the purposes of cumulative investigation, diagnoses and treatment. Obviously, the patient's confidential information will be seen by a number of administrative staff and health and social care practitioners, but each will bound by the law and the Caldicott principles, as discussed. The sharing of information is necessary for the service to function and does not constitute a breach of confidentiality.

As discussed in Chapter 5, Article 8 of the *Human Rights Act 1998* concerns the right to respect of privacy, family life home and correspondence; however, as was explained, this is a qualified right and there is a list of circumstances in which freedom from interference by a public authority can be lawfully breached.

Child protection and the prevention of abuse constitute another area in which a legitimate defence of a breach of confidence could – or should – be made. The United Kingdom is planning to introduce mandatory reporting where health and social care professionals will be legally obliged to disclose suspicion or knowledge of a child or vulnerable person suffering abuse, through the Criminal Justice Bill 2023, currently going through parliament at the time of writing. It was appalling that such a notorious figure as Jimmy Savile was allowed to abuse children and vulnerable people so blatantly and for so long, apparently with impunity. It is highly unlikely that those close to him or his victims had no knowledge or suspicion of what was occurring, but sadly some found it easier to turn their heads away rather than feel compelled to do something about the abuse. There will be serious consequences for ignoring abuse under the proposed provisions of the Criminal Justice Bill, which include a criminal offence and imprisonment of up to seven years for health and social care professionals working with children who fail to disclose knowledge or suspicion of child abuse.

Case studies

Is the following an illegitimate breach of confidentiality?

You are working as a receptionist at a town medical practice. Your next-door neighbour is one of the patients on the practice's list. You overheard someone being sick through the walls of your apartment and noticed that the woman concerned refused an alcoholic drink recently at a mutual neighbour's birthday party. You suspect your neighbour may be pregnant and are curious as she currently doesn't have a partner. You know she had a consultation with a GP recently and you have a discreet look at her medical records, to which you have access to satisfy your curiosity; however, you keep it to yourself. Is this an illegitimate breach of confidentiality?

The answer is yes. Accessing information (including care records) without good reason, permission or valid authorisation is breaking confidentiality even if you do not go on to share the information with a third party.

***

You are a teacher working in a reception class and the children are getting ready for a dance and movement session. You notice that Adam, a four year-old boy, has what looks like fingertip bruising to his upper arms. You seek a moment to have a private word with Adam and calmly ask how he got the marks you noticed on his upper arms. He said that Rob had done them when he was cross with him and had shaken him. You understand Rob to be Adam's mum's new partner. You reassure Adam and end the conversation.

Do you:

a) Ring Adam's mum to discuss the conversation you have just had with Adam?

b) Do nothing due to fear of breaching Adam's confidence?

c) Make a referral to the Children's Services branch of your local authority and give precise details of the conversation you had with Adam?

d) Make a referral to the Children's Services branch of your local authority and give precise detail of the conversation you had with Adam, then ring Adam's mum and inform her about what you have done?

e) Do nothing straight away but keep an eye on Adam over the next week to see whether he displays any further signs of concern.

f) You are unsure how best to proceed, so after the conversation with Adam you seek out the member of staff responsible for safeguarding and repeat what Adam had said.

Options (c) and (f) are appropriate here because it appears to be a child protection issue, for which a referral needs to be made to Children's Services that morning.

Options (a) and (d) are not appropriate, as you do not know whether Adam's mum has knowledge of the alleged incident of chastisement or was complicit in it or would make Adam change his story or not say anything to protect Rob.

Option (b) is inappropriate as a breach of confidence is not only legitimate but required for reasons of safeguarding and the prevention of harm.

Option (e) is inappropriate as you would be failing to refer an alleged safeguarding concern. Also, delay could result in the bruises fading and important evidence being lost.

Confidentiality: some dos and don'ts

Dos

» Familiarise yourself with your duties and responsibilities under the data protection legislation and Caldicott principles, and abide by them in your practice.

» Familiarise yourself with the duties and responsibilities of your professional body's codes of conduct in respect of confidentiality and abide by them in your practice.

» Familiarise yourself with your duties and responsibilities your employer has stipulated in the organisation's policies and procedures in information governance and abide by them in your practice.

» Regard the information you obtain about others in the course of your work as privileged information and commit to exercising care in its handling.

» If you are faced with an issue about how best to proceed regarding an issue of confidentiality, seek support/advice from a supervisor, information governance officer or Caldicott Guardian within your organisation.

» The need to describe a stressful, poignant or humorous incident experienced at work with family or friends may be understandable, but if doing so do be mindful of your responsibilities regarding confidentiality and protect the identity of patients, clients or colleagues.

Don'ts

» If you are faced with uncertainty about how best to proceed with an issue of confidentiality, don't be pressured into a hasty decision but say you need to consult someone.

» Don't make assumptions about having obtained consent to share information.

» Don't receive information on the basis of promising not to share it. You don't know what you are going to be told and if it is a disclosure about an intent to self-harm or cause harm to another person or abuse someone, or they are a victim of harm or abuse, you may have to breach confidentiality as you have a duty to do so. You could explain why you are not able to receive information on the basis of promising not to share it with anyone and encourage disclosure without such a promise, but breaking trust should be avoided.

» Don't gossip about clients, patients or colleagues.

» When taking photos with your phone, don't include people in the shot who have not given their consent for their image to be taken as this is breaking confidentiality. It is also sensible, when gaining consent, to include its proposed distribution as being limited to the friends of the photographer is different from unrestricted Facebook membership. Rachel Burns lost her 21 year-old career as a care home manager as a result of an unintended breach of confidentiality when she photographed an entertainment event at the home and posted it on Facebook. A resident appeared in the photo and could be identified. This was considered gross misconduct by her employers (McDermott and Coomes, 2017).

Conclusion

There seems to be a lot to know – or at least be aware of – quite apart from your acquisition of clinical skills and knowledge. It is, however, a vital part of your practice to apply values, ethics and rights. Your management of consent and confidentiality, although different, is comparable in importance to your clinical skills. In summary, your occupational skills consist of your values, ethics and rights, your management of consent and confidentiality, and your clinical skills.

Chapter 7 | Conclusion

In Chapter 1, through the experiments of Milgram and Zimbardo and real-life examples, we saw how all human beings have the capacity to comply with instructions we know to be wrong, behave toward others in cruel and inhuman ways and commit acts that are disrespectful to the dignity of, and harmful to, those to whom we owe a duty of care. Through exercising differentials in power and authority, we are also capable of unfairness, prejudice and discrimination. We might be tempted to acknowledge the potential to behave badly but think it unlikely that we will because we are good, well-intentioned people. This would be naïve and leave us and our careers vulnerable. Being good, well-intentioned people can offer a degree of protection against the potential for behaving badly being realised, but we are fallible and can err, so we need something to bolster and reinforce our motivation to behave with probity. The application of occupational standards and codes of conduct, the role of inspection, quality assurance and scrutiny, and the implementation of regulation and legislation all make a significant contribution to this objective. It is therefore crucial that practitioners familiarise themselves with and abide by the procedures that regulate and govern their occupation to safeguard their clients and patients, their own practice and their profession.

Chapter 1 also invited practitioners to consider what is appropriate in decisions about displaying expressions of their identity in professional practice. Some employers will offer guidelines and stipulations regarding a dress code, but the provisions of the *Equality Act 2010* allow for the exercise of some choice – for example, in displaying signs of religious identity. What you regard as appropriate may depend upon whether you regard yourself as a practitioner first when working, in which case you may adopt a neutral appearance – simply the uniform of your occupation and a lanyard conferring your ID. Those who, for example, consider themselves as a Christian first may want to display a crucifix, or a Sikh may be required to wear a turban. The decision is not solely a personal one, as our appearance can send a message or make a statement to our clients, patients and colleagues. In a multicultural society such as the United Kingdom, manifestations of difference should be tolerated and accepted, but they can also introduce otherness through the mutual identification of membership of the group being manifested (insiders) or a mutual recognition of non-membership (outsiders).

It is a professional responsibility to acquire knowledge and clinical skills required by your occupation, but it is equally important today for practitioners to hold appropriate values, ethics and an understanding of their rights, as well as those of their clients, patients and employers. In Chapter 2, values were explored. First, some consideration was given to what we mean by the word 'values', and an understanding of this was established. We then considered what values might be appropriate for a practitioner in health and social care and undertook an exercise in determining what values might be considered essential and desirable for such a worker to hold. A review of personal and professional values was undertaken, including the potential difficulties that could arise in one's professional life if there was incongruence or the lack of a good fit between the two. The chapter identified some of the regulatory bodies within the health and social care professions and alluded to the codes of conduct they publish, in which they stipulate some of the behaviour they expect their members to exhibit as registrants and the values that underpin them. Towards the end of the chapter, professional boundaries were considered and some scenarios were presented with comments about what may be an appropriate response by the practitioner to each situation. The chapter concluded in offering some basic principles for establishing a professional relationship with clients and patients.

Chapter 3 introduced some of the main schools of ethical philosophy and traditions, which provide an insight into what often underpins our perspectives about what we consider to be right or wrong and shape our views on important issues of the day. This not only helps us to understand ourselves but informs our understanding of where others may be coming from. The chapter included an important section on how the application of either Kantian or utilitarian ethics can produce different outcomes from the same presenting issue, and went onto suggest why it may be ethically advantageous to separate budget-holding responsibilities that provide services for an area from undertaking an assessment of the needs of an individual to access those services.

Chapter 4 went onto to introduce and discuss the four pillars of medical ethics, namely autonomy, non-maleficence, beneficence and justice, and considered some of the challenges involved in applying these to real-life situations. Some examples were given of the treatment of patients, in which the principles of the four pillars had been forgone, illustrating the need for ethics in medicine. The chapter also explored ethical dilemmas, specifically those arising from debates on euthanasia and eugenics and considered how different schools of ethical philosophy could inform such debates, producing different outcomes. The chapter concluded by offering a way to safeguard our professional practice by pledging the adoption of Kantian ethics in relation to our clients and patients.

Chapter 5 examined the discourse of rights, from what is meant by rights through to different sorts of rights and the circumstances that gave rise to them. Some of the significant developments in the evolution of rights, including those of the child, were identified before a more detailed description was provided of two important pieces of legislation enshrining the rights and entitlements we currently enjoy: the *Human Rights Act 1998* and the *Equality Act 2010*. A discussion of the topic of discrimination followed, including the role of rights legislation in protecting vulnerable groups from being subjected to it. Finally, a personal approach to the navigation of discrimination was offered for the reader to consider.

Chapter 6 discussed consent and confidentiality and highlighted the need for practitioners to manage these important areas of practice lawfully and in compliance with the principles and procedures that govern them. Consent where patients lack capacity was considered, as were the circumstances in which obtaining consent is not straightforward. The Caldicott principles on the management of information were introduced and the chapter concluded with some dos and don'ts for managing confidentiality appropriately.

We will now consider how you can look after yourself during the rigour of practice, not just through a term or year but throughout your career. The aim of what follows is to enable you to construct your own firewall to promote your well-being and guard against occupational burnout. The chapter will conclude with a quiz.

Surviving the occupational landscape

In addition to coping with an intellectually and emotionally demanding profession, practitioners need to manage the occupational landscape, which consists of several competing agendas. These include the way government policy – or lack of it – impacts the working environment, then how this is translated by employers in their policies and procedures, and their overall ethos. The relationship with associated agencies and their reaction to policy can also impact your working environment. Then there is how this manifests in your primary patient's or client's care. Finally, there are secondary clients (the primary client's parents or carers) and tertiary clients (the primary client's friends and extended family). For example, several previous prime ministers have said they would sort out social care, meaning to present policy to manage the dynamic of hospital discharge more efficiently to community care – either home or nursing home care– ending the problem of bed blocking, which causes major problems for bed availability in hospitals, resulting in lengthy waiting periods for patients in emergency departments and beds in hospital corridors. Despite such promises, no comprehensive policy has yet emerged, even though Andrew Dilnot was commissioned to review this problem, and to make proposals and recommendations (Dilnot, 2011). This has resulted in additional pressure being applied to the management of bed availability and impacted everyone in the chain, from ambulance staff arriving at hospitals with patients, to the staff in emergency departments managing the triage system and those awaiting admission, to the ward staff managing reduced turnaround time between patients leaving and those arriving, and the patients awaiting admission. There are no simple solutions for managing the impact of the pressure experienced from being a part of this chain. You might rely on your good interpersonal skills in managing any frustration felt by your patients or carers or colleagues, but unless you are a senior member of hospital management, in which case you might be able to exercise some influence on hospital policy, the extent to which you can bring influence to bear on these circumstances is limited.

Spheres of influence

When considering how you may best manage stress and pressure resulting from occupational practice, it is worth thinking about the extent to which you can realistically influence events. In the above example, even if you are a senior member of hospital management, your power to influence policy will be limited. You cannot, for example, impose national policy as this needs to come from the government, so you will have to manage demand using the current resources available despite inadequacies in this equation. I am not suggesting that the practitioner should become uncritically accepting of aspects of their working environment that they think could be improved, but there is little point in beating up on yourself for things beyond your power.

So, in an analysis of stress management, draw a diagram of three concentric circles. Put into the circle in the centre the things you have direct control over, one of which is how you choose to react to X or Y. In the middle circle, put those things over which you do not have direct control but where you can express some influence, even if it is just offering your opinion in a staff meeting or joining a trades union or a professional association. In the outer circle put the things over which you have no control and no realistic chance of influencing, this might be resource allocation or social policy, in which perhaps the only opportunity you have to bring influence to bear is voting in a general election for the party whose policies you find most agreeable. You might decide the issues in this outer circle are not worth stressing over, not because they do not matter but due to the lack of power you have to change them. You can then decide to reserve your energy to manage the things in the first and second circles in a manner that suits you (see Figure 7.1).

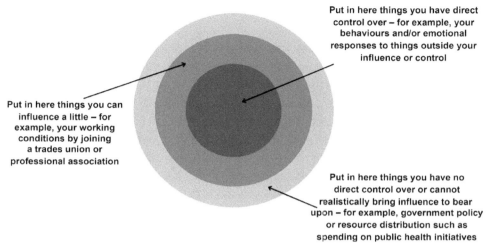

Figure 7.1 Spheres of influence

Good and bad stress

There are different types of stress, some of which is good. For example, imagine that you are due to deliver an assessed group presentation. Unless you are a very chilled-out individual, the prospect of this event is likely to cause some stress, but this is what I would describe as good stress – or performance stress that enables us to step up to the plate and perform. This contrasts with the stress caused by external pressure over which we have no or little control. I would encourage the reader to enjoy these good stress events, as they present you with opportunities to perform and do your best.

A word about whistleblowing

If you become aware of or witness practice about which you are sufficiently concerned to consider whistleblowing, you need to think about how best to do this and who to talk to about your concerns. Some organisations have a whistleblowing hotline or other means by which you can express your concerns anonymously, being known only by a unique code number to protect your identity. You are advised to consult the organisation's policy and procedures manual for information about the process. Of course, one should do the right thing, but such decisions are not easy, and consideration should be given to whether you should safeguard your identity as we know there can be unanticipated repercussions for whistleblowers. A case in point occurred in Blackpool in 2018. In 2023, nurse Catherine Hudson was jailed along with a health and social care colleague for having given unprescribed sedatives to stroke patients on their ward to have 'an easy shift'. The pair were investigated after a student nurse on a work placement at

Blackpool's Victoria Hospital witnessed events and told senior managers. The prosecution asked for the whistleblower's name not to be disclosed. Whoever they are, they are a credit to their profession (Hirst et al., 2023).

Build your firewall

In addition to those who love and care about you personally, as a health and social care practitioner you are a precious resource to the nation, your community, your employer and all those clients and patients to whom you will offer a service during your career. You have a responsibility to look after this resource and to do what you can to prevent occupational burnout. One way to do this is to build your firewall, which represents your individual set of defences that will promote and protect your sense of well-being in occupational life. It will be unique to you, although it may include activities in common with others. Building it starts with an analysis of what you need to survive occupationally. As this is different for each practitioner, it cannot be prescribed.

Exercise

» Start with a piece of flip chart paper and a marker pen, and draw a spider diagram with you in the centre and spokes extending out, at the end of which are your identified needs.

The needs you identify may be different from those I've suggested or may include some and not others, so please do not feel limited to the following, which include support, mindfulness, exercise, pleasure pastimes, holidays and annual leave, and opportunities for growth and development.

Support

Under each heading, you need to identify the type and source of what you need – for example, support. What need do you have for personal support? Then identify the sources of this support, which may be family, friends or a partner. What need do you have for emotional support? This may include clinical supervision – but what about pastoral supervision? Can you bring your agenda to this? How are the components of supervision of accountability, professional development and general support going to be met and by whom? If you have identified a need but not a source to meet that need, this will have to change. It is unlikely that a need will disappear so a source to meet it should be sought. What contingency plans can be put in place in the event of a breakdown in any of the sources of support identified?

Mindfulness

How are you going to look after your own mental health and any spiritual needs? Again, how you do this this will be unique to you, but I highlight this as a generic need without any reliance on religious belief or agnosticism, as it is perfectly possible to be a moral agent and tend to any spiritual needs as a secular atheist. You might fulfil this need by practising a particular religion or meditation or yoga, or simply being in contact with nature or places special to you. Whatever way you choose to address this need, ensure that you take some restorative time out for you.

Physical exercise is a great stress-buster, but not everyone enjoys jogging or regularly going for a workout in the gym. However, taking some exercise in addition to that undertaken at work can make an important contribution to our sense of well-being and self-esteem.

Exercise

» Decide on what works for you and consider how you are going to maintain your fitness programme or schedule of physical activity.

Pleasure pastimes

It is important to strike a balance between giving your best in an emotionally demanding occupation and spending some time doing things you enjoy and from which you derive pleasure. This could be anything from music and dance to bouldering or mountain biking. It doesn't matter what it is, so long as you enjoy it and it provides respite and guards against the pressures of your working life imposing themselves to the point where you begin to neglect fulfilling this need.

Holidays and annual leave

Linked to pleasure pastimes, it is important that you periodically take a break from work and do something different. Guard against the pressures of work encroaching on taking regular breaks as your annual leave entitlement allows.

Opportunities for growth and development

Some of us find it healthy to present ourselves with challenges occasionally, as fulfilling them provides us with a sense of achievement. I am not suggesting that

CONCLUSION

people seek promotion or take on greater responsibility within a work setting, as this is not for everyone. I am using the word 'challenge' in its wider sense. Possibilities could range from climbing a mountain to undertaking further education or learning a language or to play an instrument. You might feel you have quite enough on, as many registered occupations request registrants to maintain a portfolio evidencing continued professional development and this may be linked to other requirements such as annual appraisal. But do bear this idea in mind and if you feel it undertaking a challenge at some point could be beneficial go for it.

Now organise your spider diagram into your bespoke firewall, which not only sets out your needs to remain healthy in practice but also identifies how they will be met. Once your diagram is done, don't forget about it – display it somewhere prominent and review it periodically to ascertain how well it is working and whether any amendments are necessary. Figure 7.2 shows how I would identify my needs.

Figure 7.2 My firewall

So now you have read this book, what can you recall?

Complete this multiple-choice quiz to find out. The answers are at the end of the book.

Please circle which one of the four answers you think is correct.

1. Ethics are:

    A   The study of morals in human society

    B   A formal expression of values

    C   Concerning the rightness or wrongness of an act

    D   All of the above

2. A right is something that:

    A   You are automatically entitled to

    B   The state has agreed to do or uphold on behalf of its citizens

    C   You can claim to have earned

    D   Is shared by all human beings

3. The Enlightenment was:

    A   Another term for the Industrial Revolution

    B   A programme of installing electric lighting in domestic homes

    C   An international movement that gave birth to the modernist tradition

    D   A postmodernist idea that found favour in Scotland and parts of Europe

4. Who maintained that action should only be done through a sense of duty?

    A   John Locke

    B   John Stuart Mill

    C   William Wilberforce

    D   Immanuel Kant

5. Utilitarianism is a school of ethical philosophy that says an action is good when:

    A   It benefits the majority

    B   It benefits the ruling classes

    C   It conforms to the will of God

    D   It comes closest to striking a balance between good and bad outcomes

6. Which of the following are movements or ideas associated with radical ethics?

    A   Marx's theory of class

    B   Environmental campaigners like eco-warriors

    C   Anti-vivisectionists

    D   All of the above

7. Existentialism is a school of thought that advocates a person should:

    A   Take responsibility for themselves and their actions

    B   Arrive at decisions about what they should do in accordance with what those in authority say

    C   Allow their destiny to direct their life-course

    D   Make decisions about what they do without regards to moral philosophy

8. An example of an essentialist characteristic of our identity is:

    A   Our masculinity and femininity

    B   Our skin colour

    C   Our social class

    D   Our faith

9. An example of an intrinsic value would be:

    A   A preference for skiing holidays rather than beach holidays

    B   An appreciation of the value of your car in enabling you to get around

C   Being trustworthy

D   Chocolate

10. Working in the field of social care is itself:

    A   An amoral enterprise

    B   A moral enterprise

    C   An immoral enterprise

    D   None of the above

11. Discrimination is:

    A   Unfavourable treatment based on prejudice

    B   Basing decisions on views that conform to a fixed mental image

    C   An abuse of one's power

    D   A process to ensure proportional representation

12. Those who suppose that they can make wiser decisions than the people for whom they act are known as:

    A   Agronomists

    B   Paternalists

    C   Collectivists

    D   Recidivists

13. What is the uncomfortable feeling caused by holding conflicting beliefs and behaviours simultaneously?

    A   Cognitive disregard

    B   Cognitive disintegration

    C   Cognitive dissonance

    D   Cognitive dissociation

14. Anti-oppressive practice is where the practitioner:

    A   Ensures their practice does not oppress their client

    B   Ensures their client is treated fairly

C Positively combats any form of oppression in their practice

D Avoids practice that the client may perceive as oppressive

15. The manner in which the police investigated the murder of Stephen Lawrence was described as:

    A An exceptional example of multicultural policing

    B An example of institutional racism

    C An example of personal prejudice

    D An appropriate response to the increase in knife crime within the Black/ethnic community

16. The acronym for Thompson's model of oppression is

    A CPS

    B PSI

    C BSP

    D PCS

17. The UN Convention on Human Rights was ratified in:

    A 1927

    B 1948

    C 1963

    D 1997

18. Which one is NOT one of the 'protected characteristics' of the *Equality Act 2010*

    A Social class

    B Age

    C Race

    D Being pregnant or on maternity leave

19. Which one of the options describes an unlawful act?

    A Indirect discrimination

    B   Direct discrimination

    C   Harassment

    D   All of the above

20. The European Convention on Human Rights was brought into the UK domestic legislation through an Act of Parliament in:

    A   1973

    B   1989

    C   1998

    D   2010

21. 'Hegemony' is a term used to describe:

    A   Neighbours who get on very well

    B   The process whereby the ideas of the ruling class become the ruling ideas

    C   Financial trust fund managers

    D   How the environment influences our genes

22. In Marx's theory of social class, he described the ruling class as:

    A   The aristocracy

    B   The proletariat

    C   The bourgeoisie

    D   The plutocrats

23. Political correctness is a movement that encourages:

    A   Bigotry

    B   The sensitive use of language

    C   The use of stereotypes

    D   The compensation culture

24. Ethical standards in health and social care play an important role in:

    A   Protecting users of services

    B   Protecting staff

    C   Safeguarding the profession

    D   All of the above

25. Consent can be considered to have been obtained through:

    A   Implication

    B   Spoken agreement

    C   Written and signed agreement

    D   All of the above

26. For consent to be valid, it must be:

    A   Informed

    B   Coerced

    C   Obtained by an intermediary

    D   Witnessed

27. The Caldicott principles are used to guide practitioners on:

    A   Situations in which consent is not required

    B   Situations in which confidentially can lawfully be breached

    C   Situations in which consent should be obtained

    D   The management of information about a client

28. The Gillick principle refers to:

    A   Circumstances where a parent's consent must be sought before giving a child treatment

    B   Circumstances whereby a child could give their own consent

    C   Circumstances in which the requirement to gain consent can be waived

    D   Circumstances in which consent cannot be obtained due to lacking capacity

29. A lawful defence for breaching confidentiality exists where:

    A   It is in the public interest to do so

    B   To prevent abuse and serious harm

C   To uphold the absolute human rights of others

   D   All of the above

30. Lying to children about Santa Claus and the Tooth Fairy would be against which of the following

   A   Bentham's utilitarian ethics

   B   Kant's categorical imperative

   C   Marx's theory of class

   D   The Chinese economy

Conclusion

Spending one's working life in the service of others and being in receipt of the appreciation rightly deserved by the health and social care professions is demanding, but also a privilege. It also offers the practitioner the opportunity to maintain a balance between their own issues and those that their clients and patients are managing in their lives. This can offer the practitioner a sense of perspective regarding their place in the bigger picture.

I would like to wish you a long and fulfilling career in whatever profession within you have chosen within the rewarding field of health and social care.

Multiple-choice quiz answers

1. D
2. B
3. C
4. D
5. A
6. D
7. A
8. B
9. C
10. B
11. A
12. B
13. C
14. C
15. B
16. D
17. B
18. A
19. D
20. C
21. B
22. C
23. B
24. D
25. D
26. A
27. D
28. B
29. D
30. B

References

Agarwal, P (2020) *Sway: Unravelling Unconscious Bias.* London: Bloomsbury.

American Declaration of Independence 1776. Available at: https://history.state.gov/milestones/1776-1783/declaration#:~:text=By%20issuing%20the%20Declaration%20of,colonists'%20motivations%20for%20seeking%20independence (accessed 14 June 2024).

American Red Cross (2011) *Summary of the Geneva Conventions of 1949 and Their Additional Protocols.* Washington, DC: Red Cross. Available from: www.redcross.org/content/dam/redcross/atg/PDF_s/International_Services/International_Humanitarian_Law/IHL_SummaryGenevaConv.pdf (accessed 26 August 2023).

Banks, S (2012) *Ethics and Values in Social Work,* 2nd ed. Basingstoke: Palgrave Macmillan.

Baughan, J and Smith, A (2013) *Compassion, Caring and Communication; Skills for Nursing Practice*, 2nd ed. London: Routledge.

BBC (no date) Programmes Categorised as Religion & Ethics. Available at: www.bbc.co.uk/religion (accessed 26 May 2024).

Beauchamp, T and Childress, J (2019) *Principles of Biomedical Ethics.* New York: Oxford University Press.

Benbow, W and Jordan, G (2015) *A Handbook for Student Nurses*, 3rd ed. Banbury: Lantern.

Bentham, J (2007 [1789]) *Introduction to the Principles of Morals and Legislation.* New York: Dover Publications.

Bristol Royal Infirmary Inquiry (2001) *The Report of the Public Inquiry into Children's Heart Surgery at the Bristol Royal Infirmary 1984–1995.* Available at: www.bristol-inquiry.org.uk/final_report/the_report.pdf (accessed 14 June 2024).

British Medical Association (2024) HS Backlog Data Analysis. Available at: www.bma.org.uk/advice-and-support/nhs-delivery-and-workforce/pressures/nhs-backlog-data-analysis#:~:text=In%20the%20past%2012%20months,Emergency%20Care%20capital%20incentive%20scheme (accessed 14 June 2024).

Burn-Murdock, J (2023) FT Analysis of Data from the International Social Survey Programme, *Luxembourg Income Study*. Available at: www.lisdatacenter.org/our-data/lis-database (accessed 14 June 2024).

Caulfield, H (2005) *Accountability: Vital Notes for Nurses.* Oxford: Blackwell.

Campbell, D (2022) NHS Vacancies in England at 'Staggering' New High as Almost 10% of Posts Empty. *The Guardian*, 1 September. Available at: www.theguardian.com/society/2022/sep/01/nhs-vacancies-in-england-at-staggering-new-high-as-almost-10-of-posts-empty (accessed 14 June 2024).

Care Quality Commission (2011) *The Mental Capacity Act 2005 Guidance for providers.* Available at www.cqc.org.uk/sites/default/files/documents/rp_poc1b2b_100563_20111223_v4_00_guidance_for_providers_mca_for_external_publication.pdf (accessed 14 June 2024).

Care Quality Commission (2022) State of Care 2022/23. Available at: www.cqc.org.uk/publications/major-report/state-care/2022-2023 (accessed 14 June 2024).

Care Quality Commission (2023) *Liberty Protection Safeguards (DoLS)*. Available at: www.cqc.org.uk/publications/major-report/state-care/2022-2023/dols#:~:text=In%20April%202023%2C%20the%20government,for%20providers%20and%20local%20authorities (accessed 14 June 2024).

Care Standards Act 2000. Available at: www.legislation.gov.uk/ukpga/2000/14/contents (accessed 14 June 2024).

Cartwright Inquiry (1988) *The Report of the Cervical Cancer Inquiry, 1988.* Available at: www.nsu.govt.nz/health-professionals/national-cervical-screening-programme/legislation/cervical-screening-inquiry-0n (accessed 14 June 2024).

REFERENCES

Caulfield, H (2005) *Accountability: Vital Notes for Nurses*. Oxford: Blackwell.

Children Act 1989. Available at: www.legislation.gov.uk/ukpga/1989/41/contents (accessed 14 June 2024).

Cluskey, P (2023) Dutch Government to Ban Police Officers from Wearing Religious Symbols as Part of Uniforms in Public. *The Irish Times*, 29 June. Available at: www.irishtimes.com/world/europe/2023/06/29/dutch-government-to-ban-police-officers-from-wearing-religious-symbols-as-part-of-uniforms-in-public (accessed 14 June 2024).

Committee on Standards in Public Life (2013) *Promoting Standards in Public Life: Best Practice*. Available at: www.gov.uk/government/publications/standards-matter-thirteenth-report-of-the-committee-on-standards-in-public-life (accessed 14 June 2024).

Countryside and Rights of Way Act 2000. Available at: www.legislation.gov.uk/ukpga/2000/37/contents (accessed 14 June 2024).

Cuthbert, S and Quallington, J (2017) *Values and Ethics for Care Practice*. Banbury: Lantern.

Data Protection Act 1998. Available at: www.legislation.gov.uk/ukpga/1998/29/contents (accessed 14 June 2024).

Data Protection Act 2018. Available at: www.gov.uk/data-protection (accessed 14 June 2024).

Department of Health (2014) Winterbourne View NHS Final Report. Available at: www.england.nhs.uk/wp-content/uploads/2014/11/transforming-commissioning-services.pdf (accessed 14 June 2024).

Duncan, P (2010) *Values, Ethics and Health Care*. London: Sage.

Dilnot Commission (2011) *The Dilnot Report*. Available at: www.kingsfund.org.uk/insight-and-analysis/briefings/dilnot-commission-report-social-care (accessed 14 June 2024).

Equality and Human Rights Commission (EHRC) (2019) Direct and Indirect Discrimination. Available at: www.equalityhumanrights.com/equality/equality-act-2010/your-rights-under-equality-act-2010/direct-and-indirect-discrimination?return-url=https%3A%2F%2Fwww.equalityhumanrights.com%2Fsearch%3Fkeys%3Ddirect%2Band%2Bindirect%2Bdiscrimination (accessed 14 June 2024).

Electoral Commission (2016) Available at: www.electoralcommission.org.uk/research-reports-and-data/our-reports-and-data-past-elections-and-referendums/report-23-june-2016-referendum-uks-membership-european-union (accessed 14 June 2024).

Encyclopædia Britannica (2024) Hippocratic Oath: Ethical Code. Available at: www.britannica.com/topic/Hippocratic-oath (accessed 14 June 2024).

Equality Act 2010. Available at: www.legislation.gov.uk/ukpga/2010/15/contents (accessed 14 June 2024).

European Convention on Human Rights (1953) Available at: www.echr.coe.int/documents/d/echr/convention_ENG (accessed 14 June 2024).

Festinger, L (1957) *A Theory of Cognitive Dissonance*. Stanford, CA: Stanford University Press.

French Declaration of the Rights of Man and Citizen (1789) Available at: www.elysee.fr/en/french-presidency/the-declaration-of-the-rights-of-man-and-of-the-citizen#:~:text=History-,The%20Declaration%20of%20the%20Rights%20of%20Man%20and%20of%20the,There%20were%20many%20proposals (accessed 14 June 2024).

Galton, F (1907 [1883]) Inquiries into Human Fertility and its Development. London: J M Dent & Co.

Hawley, G (2007) *Ethics in Clinical Practice*. Harlow: Pearson Education.

The Health and Care Professions Council (HCPC) (2016) *Standards of Conduct Performance and Ethics*. London: HCPC. Available at: www.hcpc-uk.org/standards/standards-of-conduct-performance-and-ethics (accessed 14 June 2024).

The Health and Care Professions Council (HCPC) (2023) *The Standards of Proficiency for Physiotherapists*. London: HCPC. Available at: www.hcpc-uk.org/standards/standards-of-proficiency/physiotherapists (accessed 14 June 2024).

REFERENCES

The Health Foundation (2023) 2.5 Million More People in England Projected to be Living with Major Illness by 2040. London: The Health Foundation. Available at: www.health.org.uk/news-and-comment/news/25-million-more-people-in-england-projected-to-be-living-with-major-illness-by-2040 (accessed 14 June 2024).

Herring, J (2006) *Medical Law and Ethics*. Oxford: Oxford University Press.

Hirst, L, Lazaro, R and PA News (2023) Blackpool Nurse and Colleague Jailed Over Drugging Patients, *BBC News*, 15 December. Available at: www.bbc.co.uk/news/uk-england-lancashire-67706765 (accessed 14 June 2024).

Holmes, J (2021) Tackling Obesity: The Role of the NHS in a Whole-system Approach. London: The King's Fund. Available at: www.kingsfund.org.uk/insight-and-analysis/reports/tackling-obesity-nhs (accessed 14 June 2024).

Human Fertilisation and Embryology Act 1990. Available at: www.legislation.gov.uk/ukpga/1990/37/contents (accessed 14 June 2024).

Human Fertilisation and Embryology Act 2008. Available at: www.legislation.gov.uk/ukpga/2008/22/contents (accessed 14 June 2024).

Human Rights Act 1998. Available at: www.legislation.gov.uk/ukpga/1998/42/contents (accessed 14 June 2024).

Kant, I (2016 [1792]) *Fundamental Principles of the Metaphysic of Morals*, trans T. Kingsmill Abbott. London: Create Space.

The Lancet (2013) *World Report*, 381(9866). Available at: www.thelancet.com/journals/lancet/issue/vol381no9866/PIIS0140-6736(13)X6008-8 (accessed 14 June 2024).

MacPherson Inquiry (1999) *The Stephen Lawrence Inquiry*. Available at https://assets.publishing.service.gov.uk/media/5a7c2af540f0b645ba3c7202/4262.pdf (accessed 14 June 2024).

Magna Carta (1215) Available at: www.parliament.uk/magnacarta/#:~:text=Magna%20Carta%20was%20issued%20in,as%20a%20power%20in%20itself (accessed 14 June 2024).

Mangion, D (2024) 12 Notorious UK Discrimination Cases. *Skillcast*. Available at: www.skillcast.com/blog/12-notorious-uk-discrimination-cases (accessed 14 June 2024).

Martin, G, Carlson, N and Buskist, W (2010) *Psychology*, 4th ed. Harlow: Pearson.

McDermott, S and Coomes, P (2017) I Lost My Job Over a Facebook Post – was That Fair? *BBC News*. Available at: www.bbc.co.uk/news/stories-41851771 (accessed 14 June 2024).

McSherry, W, McSherry, R and Watson, R (2012) *Care in Nursing: Principles, Values and Skills*. Oxford: Oxford University Press.

Mental Capacity Act 2005. Available at: www.legislation.gov.uk/ukpga/2005/9/contents (accessed 14 June 2024).

Mental Health Act 1983. Available at: www.legislation.gov.uk/ukpga/1983/20/contents (accessed 14 June 2024).

Mid Staffordshire NHS Foundation Trust (2010) Independent Inquiry into Care Provided by Mid Staffordshire NHS Foundation Trust January 2005–March 2009, Volume I. Available at: https://assets.publishing.service.gov.uk/media/5a7c1b11e5274a1f5cc75d16/0375_i.pdf (accessed 14 June 2024).

Mid Staffordshire NHS Foundation Trust (2013) *The Mid Staffordshire NHS Foundation Trust Public Inquiry Final Report*. Available at: www.gov.uk/government/publications/report-of-the-mid-staffordshire-nhs-foundation-trust-public-inquiry (accessed 14 June 2024).

Milgram, S (1974) *Obedience to Authority: An Experimental View*. New York: Harper & Row.

REFERENCES

Mill, J S (1859) *On Liberty*. London: John W Parker and Son.

Mill, J S (2014 [1863]) *Utilitarianism*. Cambridge: Cambridge University Press.

National Health Service (NHS) (2022) Overview Consent to Treatment. Available at: www.nhs.uk/conditions/consent-to-treatment (accessed 14 June 2024).

National Health Service (NHS) (2023) Supporting Our NHS People. Available at: www.england.nhs.uk/supporting-our-nhs-people (accessed 14 June 2024).

National Health Service (NHS) (2024) *NHS Constitution* Available at: www.gov.uk/government/publications/the-nhs-constitution-for-england (accessed 14 June 2024).

NICE (2023) NICE Recommended Weight-loss Drug to be Made Available in Specialist NHS Services. Available at: www.nice.org.uk/news/article/nice-recommended-weight-loss-drug-to-be-made-available-in-specialist-nhs-services#:~:text=Our%20committee%20has%20made%20specific,about%20drug%20on%20the%20NHS.%E2%80%9D (accessed 14 June 2024).

Nolan Committee (1995) *The Nolan Principles*. Available at: www.england.nhs.uk/non-executive-opportunities/wp-content/uploads/sites/54/2021/02/The-Nolan-Principles-of-Public-Life.pdf (accessed 14 June 2024).

Nolan Committee (2013) *Standards Matter: A review of best practice in promoting good behavior in public life*. Available at: www.gov.uk/government/publications/standards-matter-a-review-of-best-practice-in-promoting-good-behavior-in-public-life (accessed 14 June 2024).

Northway, R and Hopes, P (2022) *Learning Disability Nursing*. St Albans: Critical Publishing.

Nursing & Midwifery Council (2024) *The Code: Professional Standards of Practice and Behaviour for Nurses, Midwives and Nursing Associates*. Available at: www.nmc.org.uk/standards/code (accessed 14 June 2024).

Oxfam (2011) *Haiti Investigation Final Report 2011*. Available at: https://d1tn3vj7xz9fdh.cloudfront.net/s3fs-public/haiti_investigation_report_2011.pdf (accessed 14 June 2024).

Parliamentary and Health Service Ombudsman (2011) *Care and Compassion*. London: The Stationary Office. Available at: www.ombudsman.org.uk/sites/default/files/2016-10/Care%20and%20Compassion.pdf (accessed 14 June 2024).

Percival, T (1803) *Medical Ethics; or, a Code of Institutes and Precepts, Adapted to the Professional Conduct of Physicians and Surgeons; In Hospital Practice*. London: S Russell for J Johnson.

Ploetz, A (1904) Grundlinien einer Rassenhygiene [Basic Principles of Racial Hygiene]. Berlin: S Fischer.

Royal Commission into Deep Sleep Therapy (1990) *Report of the Royal Commission into Deep Sleep Therapy*. Available at: https://catalogue.nla.gov.au/catalog/544640 (accessed 14 June 2024).

Samuriwo, R, Hannigan, B, Pattison, S and Todd, A (2018) *Values in Health and Social Care*. London: Jessica Kingsley.

Seedhouse, D (2005) *Values-Based Decision-Making for the Caring Professions*. Chichester: Wiley.

Thompson, D (1995) *Concise Oxford Dictionary*, 9th ed. Oxford: Oxford University Press.

Thompson, N (2006) *Anti-Discriminatory Practice*. London: Palgrave Macmillan.

Thompson, N (2020) *Holding onto Our Values*. London: Pavilion.

Tones, K and Green, G (2004) Health Promotion: Planning and Strategies. London: Sage.

UK Government (2024) *Infected Blood Compensation Scheme Summary*. Available at: www.gov.uk/government/publications/infected-blood-compensation-scheme-summary/infected-blood-compensation-scheme-summary (accessed 14 June 2024).

133

REFERENCES

UK Parliament (1689) Bill of Rights 1689. Available at: www.parliament.uk/about/living-heritage/evolutionofparliament/parliamentaryauthority/revolution/collections1/collections-glorious-revolution/billofrights/#:~:text=It%20is%20an%20original%20Act,known%20today%20as%20Parliamentary%20Privilege (accessed 14 June 2024).

United Nations Declaration on the Rights of the Child (1989) Available at: www.unicef.org.uk/what-we-do/un-convention-child-rights (accessed 14 June 2024).

Universal Declaration of Human Rights (1948) Available at: www.un.org/en/about-us/universal-declaration-of-human-rights (accessed 14 June 2024).

US Department of Labor (1964) Legal Highlight: The Civil Rights Act of 1964. Available at: www.dol.gov/agencies/oasam/civil-rights-center/statutes/civil-rights-act-of-1964 (accessed 14 June 2024).

Vienna Declaration (1993). Available at: www.ohchr.org/sites/default/files/vienna.pdf (accessed 14 June 2024).

Warnock, M (1970) *Existentialism.* Oxford: Oxford University Press.

Wood, A (2008) *Kantian Ethics.* Cambridge: Cambridge University Press.

Index

accountability, 25
Acts of Parliament, 13
Allitt, B, 13
American Declaration of Independence, 79
annual leave, 120
Aquinas, T, 55
autonomy, 60–2

bad stress, 118
Baudrillard, J, 58
Being and Nothingness (Sartre), 50
beneficence, 63–5
Bentham, J, 47
Bill of Rights (1689), 84
Black Lives Matter movement, 55
Bristol Heart Inquiry, 66
Bristol Royal Infirmary Inquiry, 66
British Association of Social Workers (BASW), 37
British values, 28
Burn-Murdock, J, 79

Caldicott, D F, 109
Caldicott principles, 109
Capital (Marx), 54
Care Act 2014, 50
Care Planning, Placements and Case Review Regulations 2013, 13
Care Quality Commission, 4, 13
Care Standards Act 2000, 13
carers, 16–17
Children Act 1989, 78–9
Christianity, 57
Civil Rights Act 1964, 77
cognitive dissonance, 33
The Communist Manifesto (Marx), 54
confidentiality, 106–13
　do's and don'ts, 112–13
　illegitimate breach of, 111–12
　legitimate defence breach, 109–10
　no breach of confidence, 109–10
consent, 101–6
　assessing capacity principles, 103
　challenges to expressions, 102
　children, young people and, 105–6
　informed, 102
　mental capacity, 103–4
　obtaining, 101
　oral, 102
　written, 102
consequentialist principle, 47

continuum diversity model, 97
Countryside and Rights of Way Act 2000, 78
Covid-19 pandemic, 15–16, 83
Criminal Justice Bill (2023), 110
Critique of Practical Reason (Kant), 45
Critique of Pure Reason (Kant), 45
cultural values, 31
Curry, Edwina, 28

Dalit caste, 57
Darwin, C, 71
Data Protection Act 1998, 107–9
Davenport, C, 71
deontic ethics, *see* Kantian ethics
deprivation of liberty safeguards (DoLS), 78
development opportunities, 120
Dilnot, A, 116
direct discrimination, 92
discrimination, 94–100
　direct, 92
　harassment, 92
　indirect, 92
　personal approach, 99
　positive, 93
　victimisation, 92
disputed reality, 51
duty of care, 81–2

empiricism, 53
Employment Equality (Sexual Orientation) Regulations 2003, 77
The Enlightenment, 53
Equality Act 2010, 13, 22, 36, 76–7, 87, 91–4, 114, 116
established rights, 83–4
ethics
　definition of, 45
　Kantian ethics, 45–7
　medical, *see* medical ethics
　utilitarianism, 47–8
　workplace, 49–50
eugenics, 71, 73–5
Eurocentric movement, 53
European Convention on Human Rights (1950), 85
European Court of Human Rights, 72, 77, 85
euthanasia, 73–5
existentialism, 50–2, 74
　definition, 50
　health and social care, 51

135

Existentialism is a Humanism (Sartre), 51
An Experiment with an Air Pump (Wright), 54

faith, 55–8
family values, 28
Festinger, L, 33
fitness to practise, 20–1
Ford, Neil, 2
Foucault, M, 58
Francis, Robert, 3–4
freedom of assembly and association (Article 11), 89
freedom of expression (Article 10), 89
freedom of thought, conscience and religion (Article 9), 89
French Declaration of the Rights of Man and Citizen, 85

Galton, F, 71
General Chiropractic Council, 37
General Data Protection Regulation (GDPR), 106, 108
General Dental Council, 37
General Medical Council (GMC), 17, 24, 37
General Optical Council, 37
General Osteopathic Council, 37
Geneva Conventions (1949), 11
Gillick principle, 86
good stress, 118
Groundwork of the Metaphysic of Morals (Kant), 45
growth opportunities, 120

harassment, 92
Health and Care Professions Council (HCPC), 17, 37
health and social care
　codes of conduct, standards and behaviour, 36–7
　existentialism, 51
　fitness to practise, 20–1
　humanism, 52
　NMC standards, 23–6
　professional occupations identity, 21–2
　radical ethics, 55
　regulatory bodies, 17
Health Foundation, 15
Hinduism, 57
Hippocrates, 60, 65
Holding onto our Values (Thompson), 27
holidays, 120
honest and trustworthy standards, 20
honesty, 25
human existence, 51
human rights, 84–5

Human Rights Act 1998, 17, 76, 80, 85, 87–91, 116
humanism, 52–3, 74
　definition of, 52
　health and social care, 52
humanistic organisations, 53
Hunt, Jeremy, 4

illegitimate breach of confidentiality, 111–12
indirect discrimination, 92
individualism, 53
informed consent, 102
integrity, 24
interplay, 32
Introduction to the Principles of Morals and Legislation (Bentham), 47
Islam, 57

Jefferson, T, 79
justice, 65

Kant, I, 45
Kantian ethics, 45–7, 73
　applications of principles, 47
　categorical imperative, 46
　criterion of, 46
　experimental study, 49
　workplace, 49–50
Kierkegaard, S, 50
King, E, 72
Knight, H, 64
Ku Klux Klan, 12

leadership, 25
legal rights, 80
legitimate defence breach of confidentiality, 109–10
Letby, L, 13
liberty protection safeguards (LPS), 78
limitation on use of restrictions on rights (Article 18), 90
Lyotard, J F, 58

Magna Carta (1215), 78, 84
Major, J, 28
Marx, K, 54
Maslow, A, 52
medical ethics, *see also* ethics
　beneficence, 63–5
　ethical considerations/reasons, 65–6
　ethical dilemmas, 67–73
　eugenics, 71, 73–5
　euthanasia, 73–5
　justice, 65
　nonmaleficence, 62–3

overview of, 60
respect for autonomy, 60
Mendel, G, 71
Mental Capacity Act 2005, 61, 78, 103–4
Mental Health Act 1983, 78
Mental Health Act 2005, 72
Milgram, S, 9
Mill, J S, 47
mindfulness, 120
modernism, 53–4, 74
moral rights, 80

National Human Genome Research Institution, 71
National Institute for Health and Care Excellence (NICE), 64, 83
Natural law, 55
Nausea (Sartre), 51
non-maleficence, 62–3
Nursing and Midwifery Council (NMC), 5, 17, 23–6, 37

objectivity, 25
OFSTED, 13
On Liberty (Mill), 47
openness, 25

The Pale Blue Dot (Sagan), 52
palliative care, 56
paramountcy principle, 78
paternalism, 64
PCS model, 97
Percival, T, 60
performance stress, 118
person-centred counselling, 52
person-centred response, 16
personal values, 32–5
physical exercise, 120
pleasure, 120
Ploetz, A, 72
positive discrimination, 93
positive rights, 80
postmodernism, 58, 74
Principles of Biomedical Ethics (Beauchamp and Childress), 60
professional boundaries, 37–44
professional occupations identity, 21–2
professional values, 32–5
prohibition of discrimination in the enjoyment of rights and freedoms (Article 14), 90
prohibition of punishment without law (Article 7), 88
prohibition of slavery, servitude and forced/compulsory labour (Article 4), 88
prohibition of the abuse of rights (Article 17), 90
prohibition of torture/inhuman/degrading treatment/punishment (Article 3), 88

Racial Hygiene (Ploetz), 72
radical ethics, 54–5, 74
reasonable adjustments, 76
regulatory bodies, 17
religious belief, 55–8
respect for autonomy, 60
restrictions on political activity of non-nationals (Article 16), 90
right(s)
    definition of, 76
    duty of care, 81–2
    established, 83–4
    human, 84–5
    legal, 80
    moral, 80
    need for, 77–8
    positive, 80
    reasonable adjustments, 76
    responsibilities and, 82–3
    right to a fair trial (Article 6), 88
    right to family life (Article 8), 61
    right to liberty and security of the person (Article 5), 88
    right to life (Article 2), 88
    right to marry and found a family according to national laws (Article 12), 90
    right to respect for privacy and family life, home and correspondence (Article 8), 89
    self-evident, 78–9
    valid, 79
Rogers, C, 52
Royal Pharmaceutical Society, 37

Sagan, C, 52
Sartre, J-P, 50, 99
scientific knowledge, 53
secularism, 54
self-evident rights, 78–9
selflessness, 24
Shipman, H, 13
social learning theory, 31
standards of conduct, performance and ethics, 19
standards of proficiency, 18–20
Standards in public life, 24
Sunak, R, 82

Thompson, N, 27, 97
toleration, 53

UN Convention on Human Rights, 77
UN Convention on the Rights of the Child, 85–7
unconscious bias, 21
uniformity, 54
United Nations General Council (1948), 85
Universal Declaration of Human Rights, 85
Universal Declaration on the Rights of the Child (1989), 80
utilitarian ethics, *see* utilitarianism
utilitarianism, 47–8
   applications of principles, 48
   consequentialist principle, 47
   critics of, 48
   experimental study, 49
   workplace, 49–50
Utilitarianism (Mill), 47

valid rights, 79
values
   British, 28
   codes of conduct, standards and behaviour, 36–7
   cultural, 31
   definition of, 27
   family, 28
   interplay, 32
   outcomes, 30
   patients behaviour, 35–6
   personal, 32–5
   professional, 32–5
   professional boundaries, 37–44
   social learning theory, 31
victimisation, 92
Vienna Declaration and Programme of Action (1993), 85

whistleblowing, 118
working environment, 14–16
workplace ethics, 49–50
World Conference on Human Rights, 85
Wright, J, 54
written consent, 102

Yesilgoz, D, 22

zero tolerance approach, 36
Zimbardo, P, 9